PAULI MURRAY
&
CAROLINE WARE

Forty Years of Letters in Black and White

Edited by ANNE FIROR SCOTT

The University of North Carolina Press

Chapel Hill

Set in Minion type by Keystone Typesetting, Inc.

Manufactured in the United States of America

This volume was published with the assistance of the Greensboro
Women's Fund of the University of North Carolina Press.

Founding Contributors:

Linda Arnold Carlisle, Sally Schindel Cone, Anne Faircloth,
Bonnie McElveen Hunter, Linda Bullard Jennings,
Janice J. Kerley (in honor of Margaret Supplee Smith),
Nancy Rouzer May, and Betty Hughes Nichols.

The paper in this book meets the guidelines for permanence and
durability of the Committee on Production Guidelines for Book
Longevity of the Council on Library Resources.

Library of Congress Cataloging-in-Publication Data

Murray, Pauli, 1910–1985.

Pauli Murray and Caroline Ware : forty years of letters in black and white /
edited by Anne Firor Scott.

p. cm. — (Gender and American culture)

Includes bibliographical references and index.

ISBN-13: 978-0-8078-3055-0 (cloth : alk. paper)

ISBN-10: 0-8078-3055-0 (cloth : alk. paper)

1. Murray, Pauli, 1910–1985—Correspondence. 2. Ware, Caroline F. (Caroline Farrar),
1899–1990—Correspondence. 3. Women social reformers—United States—
Correspondence. 4. Women college teachers—United States—Correspondence.
5. African American women civil rights workers—Correspondence. 6. Women
historians—United States—Correspondence. 7. Feminists—United States—
Correspondence. 8. Women intellectuals—United States—Correspondence. I. Ware,
Caroline F. (Caroline Farrar), 1899–1990. II. Scott, Anne Firor, 1921–   III. Title. IV. Title:
Forty years of letters in black and white. V. Series: Gender & American culture.

HQ1412.A87 2006

305.42092′273—dc22   2006014020

10 09 08 07 06 5 4 3 2 1

In memory of

ANDREW SCOTT, 1922–2005,

and to the six who were the light of his life:

John, Thomas, Will, Sarah, Paxton, and Abby

⊀ CONTENTS

A section of photographs appears following page 112.

This book is built on an exchange of letters between two remarkable women, Pauli Murray, black, born in 1910, raised in segregated North Carolina, and Caroline Farrar Ware, white, born in 1899, raised in Massachusetts.

This project began by chance. A meeting at the Schlesinger Library in Cambridge, Massachusetts, ended unexpectedly early, and I found myself with some free hours in a manuscript collection. Brer Rabbit in the briar patch couldn't have been much happier.

Murray's life, as she told it in her autobiographies, had long intrigued me, and here was a chance to see the documents on which they were based. As I scanned the guide to the voluminous Pauli Murray collection, the name of Caroline Ware—a woman I had known and admired for many years—caught my eye. Curiosity overcame me: I sent for Box 101, and there they were, folder after folder, both sides of a correspondence that began in 1943 and ended only with Murray's death in 1985.

I had met Lina Ware, as she was called by family and friends, in 1964 when I was appointed to Lyndon Johnson's Advisory Council on the Status of Women, a follow-up to the President's Commission of the same name, chaired by Eleanor Roosevelt, on which Ware had also served. We found ourselves on the same side of many issues, and after my second council meeting she took me home to spend the night, meet her husband, Gardiner Means, and hear her outline the dynamics of the group.

This encounter led to a friendship between our families; we were often at The Farm, the place Lina and Gardiner had bought in the 1930s near Vienna, Virginia. These visits were unfailingly interesting. Lina was direct, intelligent, and highly competent at whatever she did. Gardiner talked theory with my husband and helped our seventeen-year-old design an economics project. Both had a gift for putting guests at ease and making them feel like old and valued friends.

Pauli Murray I never met, but our paths had crisscrossed in intriguing ways. In addition to our shared attachment to the Ware-Means family, in 1958 my family had moved to Orange County, North Carolina, where Murray's forebears had settled just after the Civil War. Then in 1961

I began teaching in her hometown of Durham. Lina Ware gave me a copy of *Proud Shoes* and wrote Pauli about my 1970 book on southern women. Still later, Lina wrote me about the course in women's history that Pauli was teaching at Brandeis University.

Crisscross though we did, the fundamental division of race meant that her life was inevitably different from mine, as it was different from Lina Ware's. It was the laws and attitudes that made this difference that Murray took it upon herself to challenge again and again—in the courts, in letters, in books, in confrontations of many kinds, beginning when she was very young and continuing to the end of her life. In their different but overlapping struggles for justice, Ware and Murray became lifelong allies and personal friends. From the letters it is clear that both women were part of what historians are now calling "the long civil rights movement."[1]

The friendship makes quite a story. A white Boston Brahmin with a Harvard Ph.D., an admired historian, community organizer, and consumer advocate, and a black woman, raised in poverty in the Jim Crow South, who became, over time, a writer, poet, lawyer, university professor, and the first black woman to be ordained in the Protestant Episcopal Church, writing to each other, with candor and affection, over more than forty years.

Learning about the complexities of that alliance across the racial divide, and learning far more than I had known about both these women, has been a remarkable three-year adventure. Seeing through their eyes a part of the American past that was also an important part of my own past, I was hooked.

As I began reading their thoughts about race and their spontaneous reactions to public events over four decades, I was constantly surprised to discover that most white people I asked had never heard of Murray; I was startled to discover that Ware, too, whom I believed to be one of the leading Americans of her generation—she had been well known in the years of this correspondence—was unknown even to my contemporaries, much less to the young. As I read, I was seized with the historian's version of missionary zeal: I wanted to introduce both women to a wider audience.

1. See Jacquelyn Dowd Hall, "The Long Civil Rights Movement and the Political Uses of the Past," *Journal of American History* 91, no. 4 (March 2005): 1233–63, for a thorough discussion of this concept.

Of course to do that properly would require full-scale biographies, which is not an undertaking for an octogenarian. Fortunately, at least three younger scholars are working toward biographies of Pauli Murray. As far as I can discover, only one scholar has even considered making a study of Caroline Ware.[2] Perhaps these letters, and the biographical/historical sketch that accompanies them, will encourage others to examine her life.

On the one hand, letters written in the midst of events, not intended for any eye but that of the recipient, have the obvious advantage that, unlike memories, they are not constantly revised. On the other hand, I have been aware, as the reader will be, of the limitations of letters as a historical source. Letter writers have an image of the particular person to whom they write, and while there is value in their unguarded nature, it is clear, from even a brief examination of the voluminous papers left by each of these two, that large and important parts of their lives do not appear in their correspondence with each other. In addition, important elements of their relationship are lost to the record because they were often together, and, when apart, they made good use of the telephone.

Advice to writers of fiction is always "show, don't tell." Though I yearn for the novelist's skill to bring these characters to life, I am comforted to think that, as they wrote, Pauli Murray and Caroline Ware painted their own portraits.

Editorial Note

These letters are preserved in files created by Pauli Murray herself and deposited in the Schlesinger Library of the Radcliffe Institute of Advanced Study in Cambridge, Massachusetts. Murray typed nearly all of her letters, and kept carbon copies, but few are signed. Caroline Ware, though she had, and often used, a typewriter, for some reason wrote most of her letters by hand, apparently confident that her not-always-decipherable handwriting would be decoded. Her letters are usually signed. From the whole number I chose somewhat more than half of the

---

2. Ellen Fitzpatrick, "Caroline F. Ware and the Cultural Approach to History," *American Quarterly* 43, no. 2 (June 1999): 173–98, is a beginning.

letters, those that struck me as particularly revealing, and transcribed them myself, keeping idiosyncratic spelling and diction intact.

I have omitted a good deal of ephemera and trivia. Words, sentences, and paragraphs that I have chosen to leave out are indicated by ellipses enclosed in brackets. Ellipses without brackets appeared in the original letters.

Happily the originals are available for inspection by anyone curious about the omitted letters or parts of letters. Murray's papers also include what I here call "her journal." This term covers a number of different kinds of notes kept from the mid-1930s on. Some are in regular journal-type books. Others are on loose sheets of foolscap or on legal size pads. For her trip to Ghana she was given a beautiful bound journal with her name on the cover. She kept copious records of the trip itself, but left the rest of the book blank. Writing was her way of dealing with anxiety—and she was often anxious. Sometimes there are three or four entries for a single day.

Since both women had lived several decades before they met, I have set the stage with what I have so far discovered about their lives before 1942. For this purpose I relied on several interviews that each gave at various points in her life, on some searching through their papers, and on information and impressions from people who knew them.[33] Murray wrote a family history and an autobiography. Possibly because of her legal training, both are closer to what the contemporary record confirms than are many memoirs. It must be said, however, that anyone who studies her papers will be struck by a number of revealing omissions in *Song in a Weary Throat*, the autobiography published after her death.

3. See Susan Ware, interview with Caroline Ware, January 27–29, 1982, Women in Federal Government Project, Schlesinger Library of the Radcliffe Institute for Advanced Study, Cambridge, Mass. A transcript of the interview is available at the library. There are a number of other interviews in Ware's papers at the Franklin D. Roosevelt Library in Hyde Park, but this one is more revealing than any of those. Murray was interviewed over and over. One of the best interviews was done for the Southern Oral History Program at the University of North Carolina at Chapel Hill, conducted by Genna Rae McNeil in 1975 when Murray was sixty-five (Southern Oral History Program, Collection no. 4007, Southern Historical Collection, Wilson Library, University of North Carolina at Chapel Hill).

Ware, though she tried several times, simply could not, by her own report, find the right angle from which to write about herself. That she did not preserve much in the way of personal evidence makes the letters to Murray all the more significant.

Footnotes identify people who may no longer be remembered and issues that, though they much engaged the writers, may also have vanished from memory. A project such as this reminds one of the ephemeral nature of the compelling political discourse of any time and of how little even well-informed citizens understand about important events, at a given moment, compared to what will eventually be revealed.

One more point: the Murray Papers have been purged, by Murray herself or by her family. Pages are torn from her journal, words are blacked out, and letters are referred to that cannot be found. What appear to be long gaps in the correspondence may sometimes be the result of someone's decision to remove letters.

Pauli Murray and Caroline Ware

Born and Raised in New England

Lina Ware reached adulthood at the end of the First World War—at the close of what the British historian Eric Hobsbawm once called "the long nineteenth century." She grew up in Brookline, Massachusetts, in a family of New England Unitarians with a long tradition of social concern as well as of attachment to Harvard University. Her great grandfather, Henry Ware, as dean of the Harvard Divinity School, had been both praised and vilified when he moved that institution into the Unitarian fold. Her grandfather, father, brother, and various cousins were all graduates of Harvard College. During the Civil War her grandfather, then a young college graduate, had gone with his sister to work with newly freed people in Port Royal, South Carolina, the first area to be liberated by the Union army. When President Kennedy created the Peace Corps, Ware was reminded of her grandfather's experience.

Lina Ware admired her parents. Her father—a lawyer, municipal judge, and member of the Brookline town meeting—she remembered as a generous man of gentle and just spirit with a ready sense of humor. Her mother was a busy community volunteer involved with Girl Scouts, the church, and other community organizations. Her down-to-earth view was that the most you could do for your children was to love them and keep their galoshes on. Lina had some of each parent in her makeup.

She remembered a happy, somewhat sheltered, childhood in a family where she felt loved and free to be a nonconformist. Late in her life she claimed that even as a child she noticed the division in her Brookline neighborhood between the group she labeled "top of the hill"—professional and business Protestants—and "bottom of the hill"—Irish Catholic blue-collar workers. By the time she articulated that memory she had been involved in labor activism and worker education for years.

The Ware family believed in educating women. After a few years in local private schools, in 1915 Lina and a group of her classmates, almost whimsically, chose Vassar over the more intellectually oriented Bryn Mawr. For her, it turned out to be a good choice. Under the influence of

Lucy Maynard Salmon, an extraordinary history teacher, Lina learned to use primary sources, to pay attention to the lives of ordinary people, and to think for herself. She said that Salmon students could be recognized by their careful, methodical research and spirit of inquiry. Salmon believed that nothing could be considered the final truth about the past and that knowledge should be used as the basis for "responsible conduct."[1] Many members of the Vassar faculty shared this view. Ware remembered Dean Mildred Thompson, a historian, meeting her on campus at the 1920 graduation, and saying: "Now, Lina, DO something in the world."

In light of this spirit, it is not surprising that, the day after that graduation, Lina went south for the first time, to teach in a summer school in the mountains of Kentucky. At eighty-four, she looked back to that trip as her first encounter with segregation.

Fall found her teaching at the Baldwin School in Pennsylvania, founded in 1888 to prepare girls for admission to Bryn Mawr College. From the beginning, the school was as serious about learning as the college for which it prepared students.[2]

The following summer Ware volunteered at the Bryn Mawr Summer School for Women Workers, an institution created in 1921, largely by Hilda Worthington Smith. Smith thought women workers needed more than vocational training. The Summer School was a remarkable experiment in teaching liberal arts courses to factory workers, many of whom had no more than a sixth-grade education. The students tended to teach the faculty at least as much as the faculty taught them.[3] Ware would teach worker education classes from time to time for the rest of her life. Hilda Smith, whom she called Jane, became a lifelong friend and, like Lucy Salmon, helped shape Lina Ware's pedagogy. A report she turned in

1. Notes for Lucy Salmon Panel held at Vassar, December 12, 1985, Caroline F. Ware Papers, Box 167, Folder 27, Franklin D. Roosevelt Library, Hyde Park, N.Y.

2. On the general spirit of Bryn Mawr College, see Helen Horowitz, *The Power and Passion of M. Carey Thomas* (New York: Alfred A. Knopf, 1994).

3. See R. Bauman, "Blue Collars and Bluestockings: The Bryn Mawr Summer School for Women Workers 1921–1938," in *Sisterhood and Solidarity: Workers' Education for Women, 1914–1984*, ed. Joyce Kornbluh and Mary Frederickson (Philadelphia: Temple University Press, 1984), 107–45.

some years later after a stint teaching women workers in North Carolina is revealing:

> The most striking thing is the speed with which so elementary a group was able to achieve the impressive stage of development that the girls displayed at the labor conference and in the economics class discussions during the latter part of the third week [...]. Moreover, I think it was apparent from the girls who spoke during the various discussions in the conference which I heard, that what they have acquired is not a pattern which has been superimposed on them and is likely to slip away, but something which is an integral part of themselves. Specific points learned in the various classes will go, but the ability to confront their problems and analyze them is, as far as it goes, there to stick.[4]

In her second year at Baldwin, Ware won a Vassar scholarship to study at Oxford—a rare opportunity for a woman in 1922. While at Oxford, she wrote a letter to a close friend, Helen Lockwood, that describes the life of a woman student there and gives evidence of the adventurous spirit and lively sense of humor that remained with Lina all her life (see Appendix).

Ware's time at Oxford ended unexpectedly after only one year when her mother fell ill and she was needed at home. Back in Massachusetts, contemplating her future, she decided to enroll at Radcliffe to earn a Ph.D. in economic history, and as a graduate student she worked with Harvard faculty. Wanting very much to study with Frederick Jackson Turner, she talked her way into what would turn out to be his final Harvard seminar. Though she learned a great deal from Turner, her greatest debt was to Edwin Gay, who pointed her toward a recent acquisition by the Harvard Business School of important unexamined records dealing with early experiments in the factory production of cotton cloth. She went to work studying the records as a foundation for her dissertation with characteristic enthusiasm and diligence, and the ability to see further into a subject than her predecessors had done.

Graduate school life was not all work. Lina met a young man four years her senior named Gardiner Means, who, trained as a pilot in the

---

4. Caroline Ware to Louise McLaren, August 3, 1937, Box 162, Ware Papers, FDR Library.

Great War, had found himself helping to organize postwar relief in Turkey. Supervising a village inhabited by 1,000 orphans who were working to support themselves, he observed a production process that fitted Adam Smith's explanation of supply and demand. He began to think about the contrast between the home-based production characteristic of the Turkish village and the beginnings of factory production in his own country. Returning to New England, he created a successful factory producing very fine, luxury blankets. He realized that his enterprise did not fit Smith's theories since by producing a unique product he could set prices as he pleased. He moved to Cambridge to see whether the Harvard Business School might provide the tools with which he could analyze the implications of this difference. This was the beginning of his lifelong effort to understand what he called "administered prices."

Judging by his later life, Gardiner Means liked people with ideas who were willing to argue with him. What luck, then, to meet an attractive young woman writing about a subject so close to his own interests. Late in life Ware told an interviewer a well-honed and revealing story about their courtship:

> There was an eclipse of the sun, and Gardiner invited me to drive down to Providence [. . .] where the eclipse would be total. It was icy, snowy, absolutely awful, awful driving. Gardiner had started life as an airplane pilot, and when you skid in an automobile it feels a little as if you were flying, and so he was skidding down that road, and we were arguing about this, that and the other and he managed to skid into somebody [. . .] we tried to help [. . .] but they wouldn't think of riding with us [. . .] we saw the eclipse but on the way down we got into an argument about the meaning of the words estuary and delta. One of us thought that both words applied to the land, and one that both words applied to the water. So on the way back we stopped in the Providence public library, and it turned out that one of us was half right and the other half right so that made us decide that after all we could go on [. . .].[5]

5. Susan Ware, interview with Caroline Ware, January 27–29, 1982, Women in Federal Government Project, Schlesinger Library of the Radcliffe Institute for Advanced Study, Cambridge, Mass., 34–35.

They were married in 1927 by a practically illiterate town clerk whose mind was so much on a fishing trip he planned that he nearly forgot his appointment to perform the ceremony.

In 1929 Ware's dissertation, which had been completed on time, thanks to a good deal of practical help from Gardiner, won the substantial Hart-Schaffner-Marx Prize, established to encourage scholarship in economic and commercial subjects. The judges who made the award were among the best-known economists in the country. She moved expeditiously to transform the thesis into a book, and two years later Houghton-Mifflin brought out *The Early New England Cotton Manufacture: A Study in Industrial Beginnings*. The argument of the book is now so much the conventional wisdom that present-day historians have difficulty understanding just how pathbreaking it was in the 1920s and 1930s. She argued that the entrepreneurs who created the early New England textile mills were the pioneers of the system that changed forever the nature of production and foreshadowed the dominant corporation of the future. "This industry," she wrote, "brought the factory system to the United States and furnished the laboratory wherein were worked out the industrial methods characteristic of the nation."[6] She thought that historians had not begun to understand the social and political consequences of that change, or its effect on the lives of ordinary people. She also introduced subjects at the time untouched by American historians: the nature of work culture and the multiple effects of factories on women's lives.

The book was reviewed more widely than is customary for such monographs: reviews appeared in the *New York Times* and *The Nation*, for example, as well as in the *American Economic Review*. Several reviewers recognized the originality of her approach to familiar material.

By the time Ware's book came out, Gardiner Means had moved on to Columbia University, where he was not only finishing a Ph.D. in economics but also embarking upon a research project with Adolph Berle, a friend from his army days. Together they began to write *The Modern Corporation and Private Property*, a book that would lead to a fundamen-

---

6. Caroline F. Ware, *The Early New England Cotton Manufacture: A Study in Industrial Beginnings* (Boston: Houghton Mifflin, 1931), 3.

tal change in the concept of property in American economic thought and would make both authors famous.[7]

Reading the two books together it is not difficult to envision many conversations and exchanges of work-in-progress between their authors. Their research dovetailed in interesting ways.

In 1931, in order to join Means in New York, Ware took leave from Vassar, where she had been teaching since 1925, and undertook a community study of Greenwich Village inspired by the Lynds' *Middletown*.[8] She produced a book that had little to do with the popular image of "the Village" as the home of bohemian artists and writers and a great deal to do with the culture of Italian, Irish, Spanish, and Jewish immigrants who made up the larger part of the population. Like the New England textile book, *Greenwich Village* broke new ground, both in the questions Ware asked and the data she used. It was a young person's book—her prejudices were sometimes visible—but its sources and methods, and her attention, as in her first book, to the life experience of hitherto invisible people foreshadowed a new kind of social history that would not be widely practiced by historians for another two or three decades.[9]

By 1933 the Great Depression was reaching its nadir, Franklin Roosevelt had been elected, and numbers of bright and ambitious young people had converged on Washington to take part in the president's effort to save the country from economic disaster. Gardiner Means, who had worked in Roosevelt's campaign, went to Washington to work on economic and consumer problems for the Department of Agriculture. Lina Ware, by that time a highly respected member of the Vassar faculty, spent more and more time in Washington. It was an exciting place for young professionals. Pulled into the orbit of the New Deal, with Gardiner's help and that of his mentor, Mary Harriman Rumsey, Ware, too, found a job in the Department of Agriculture. In short order she found herself

7. Adolph Berle and Gardiner C. Means, *The Modern Corporation and Private Property* (New York: Columbia University Press, 1932).

8. Robert S. Lynd and Helen Merrell Lynd, *Middletown: A Study in Contemporary Culture* (New York: Harcourt Brace, 1929).

9. Caroline F. Ware, *Greenwich Village* (New York: Columbia University Press, 1935).

helping to develop a field labeled "consumer affairs" that was just then taking shape in the federal government.

The concept of "consumer" had broadened considerably since it was developed by Florence Kelley and others at the turn of the century. Then the idea was that consumers could improve the lot of the poor by refusing to buy goods produced by ill-paid and exploited workers. The New Deal use of the term incorporated this earlier idea but added the view that consumers themselves needed protection from the greed or the neglect of local governments. Workers, it was argued, should be guaranteed certain rights to health care, decent housing, and living wages. It followed that consumers should be represented in New Deal agencies on a plane of equality with business and labor.

After Pearl Harbor this idea became focused on war workers, whose needs were manifold, including such things as decent housing, schools, and child care; medical services; and—in the case of African Americans— equal opportunity for war-created jobs.

Ware may have taken this job because she wanted to join the fun in Washington, but since thoroughness and the need to understand were among her basic characteristics, she became deeply engaged with the problems of consumer protection. In the shifting terrain of New Deal agencies she moved from one place to another battling the indifference or outright antagonism of old-line bureaucrats and the representatives of business and labor. She worked with her usual intelligence and diligence and soon became "the person to call" for any group wanting to promote consumer protection. The work introduced her to the ways and means of getting things done in Washington, knowledge she would use in the ensuing decades, both as a historian and as a practical activist. Many years later, in a long interview, she reflected with amusing insight on what she had learned about the ways of Washington seen both from inside government and from outside as a lobbyist.[10]

She stressed the importance of homework. She believed in knowing more than anyone else about any question under consideration and observed that with enough knowledge it was possible to exercise considerable power, even from a subordinate position. She had learned the importance of turf and the need to respect that of other people while

10. Susan Ware, interview with Caroline Ware, 56–57.

guarding one's own. She understood that bureaucratic processes exist in private as well as in public settings. She observed that low-level people often seem obstructionist because that is the only way they can get attention. She suggested that the use of grants and contracts led to fragmentation of responsibility and authority. She noticed the common problem that people at the center of power are often not well informed about what is going on out in the field.

In 1936, for $7,000, Ware and Means bought approximately seventy acres of land in Vienna, then a rural community in northern Virginia. They moved into an old log cabin that had been the planter's house on a small plantation and began to shape the idiosyncratic careers they would follow for the rest of their long lives. Like many of their colleagues, Ware and Means had come to Washington temporarily—and stayed for a lifetime. Each developed a multilayered life. Gardiner Means was more and more attracted to the possibility of influencing public policy, which he did both inside and outside the government. While economic theory and the search for effective public policy were the central threads of his intellectual life, he was also much concerned with putting practical ideas into action. He was an inventive entrepreneur who in time created a business raising and selling a newly developed grass, called zoysia, and soon found that he could not raise enough of the grass to keep up with demand. Later he developed what he hoped would be a program to increase employment in a depressed coastal town in Maine close to the island where he and Lina spent summers. He liked to invent things that would make life easier for the user, such as a solar cookstove inspired by cooking methods he witnessed among rural families in India.

By frugal living, the couple kept themselves free to take on the jobs they wanted to do and avoided the trap of having to do things solely for money. Family resources and their own earnings allowed them to be generous to people they thought promising who needed a hand.

The tight-knit group of early New Dealers carried on what amounted to an ongoing seminar at The Farm, and many of FDR's experiments were hatched in its living room or on its lawn. Many years later Pauli Murray recalled the spirit of the place:

> For half a century the Ware-Means home, known to friends as The Farm, has been a sanctuary for city-weary students and government

workers, intercontinental travelers on diplomatic missions, writers, professionals, and leaders of various humanitarian causes—as well as flocks of migratory birds [. . .] they lived simply in a white clapboard house overlooking rolling fields [. . .]. The center of their house, a community living room, was built as a log cabin in the 1760s, and its original beams survived. A wall of books and a huge stone fireplace where Lina broiled steaks over hot coals for Saturday night dinners were the room's dominating features.[11]

Gardiner and Lina combined their intellectual pursuits with rugged outdoor life. At one time they raised sheep, and during the winter a weekend visitor might be pressed into service rescuing newborn lambs from snow [. . .]. A visitor was free to disappear with a book [. . .] or to join in the physical chores as a FIBUL (Skipper's acronym for "Free Intelligent But Unskilled Labor") painting the barn, cutting and stacking wood, pulling up weeds [. . .][12]

Very early on, Ware and Means recognized how much shaping public policy depended on knowing who had vital information and who had the ability to get things done. They were adept at finding such people.

Ware appeared to have been born with a gift for friendship, and over her life had friends of many kinds. In her thirties she had already managed to meet with an astonishing number of the movers and shakers of those heady days. Means, by contrast, tended to be so preoccupied with the analysis of economic problems that he did not seek social contact unless it involved serious policy talk, though he was gracious to the variety of people Ware invited to come to The Farm—for a meal or for a week. She encouraged visitors and several times took in young people who were in need of housing or mentoring. Many of her letters to a wide variety of people closed with an urgent invitation to visit.

In the midst of such a busy life Ware's interest in history did not diminish. In 1939 she was asked (by an all-male committee) to organize

11. Pauli Murray, *Song in a Weary Throat: An American Pilgrimage* (New York: Harper and Row, 1987), 199–200. As a participant, years later, in occasions of the sort to which Murray refers, I was always astonished by the way Lina could broil steaks and serve them without causing any break in the ongoing, intense conversation.

12. Ibid., 198–99.

for publication a series of papers presented at the annual meeting of the American Historical Association. The result was *The Cultural Approach to History*. Ware wrote the introductory essay, which codified the kind of history that she had begun writing a decade earlier, but was only then beginning to attract interest in the discipline at large. Even in 2005 that essay is still a "place to begin" for graduate students intent on writing social history, labor history, or women's history.[13] The essay is notable for, among other things, the lucid discussion of what is now called "the problem of objectivity." With too much optimism, Ware believed that historians had come to recognize their biases and their unconscious major premises.

The voluminous correspondence growing out of Ware's government responsibilities (preserved at the FDR Library in Hyde Park, New York) shows that by 1941 she was already a person to whom others turned for advice and assistance when they needed a job, or simply needed career guidance. She often went to some lengths to be helpful to people whom she barely knew. She was also getting a good bit of fan mail for her speeches and books.

While she taught history part time at Sarah Lawrence and at American University, Ware moved from one consumer advocacy position to another as the demands of the economy and the visible approach of world war, and then war itself, led to new agencies and new challenges. She appeared regularly to testify at congressional hearings on consumer issues.

In 1940 the president appointed a National Defense Advisory Commission with members representing business, labor, agriculture, and consumers. Ware was appointed deputy to the consumer representative, Harriet Elliott, a friend and co-worker in the American Association of University Women. It soon became apparent that the other members of the commission took a dim view of the whole idea of including consumers in the focus of their work as well as a dim view of women commissioners. They made their feelings clear in unkind comments and

13. Caroline F. Ware, ed., *The Cultural Approach to History* (New York: Columbia University Press, 1940). The request came to her at a time when women scholars were not well treated by most members of the historical establishment. Ware's superior mind seems to have made an impression on the men who directed the discipline.

in such actions as forbidding the women to use the Executive Dining Room, to which the men went for lunch, and failing to include Elliott in policy discussions. In later life Ware had a number of wry stories about the things that had been said to her—without apparent embarrassment—by their male opponents. The man in charge of setting up the commission, for example, told her "if you think your commissioner is going to get the same treatment as the head of General Motors [. . .] you have another guess coming."[14] Ware was ready to fight for equal rights. Elliott, who had been a dean at North Carolina College for Women, was a "proper" southern woman who had her own ways of dealing with men. She declined to make an issue of the discrimination.

At the same time the commission's consumer division acquired more and more responsibility: for overseeing housing of war workers, welfare of children, making sure of an adequate food supply in war production neighborhoods, assuring the availability of medical care, and the like. Overworked as they were, Elliott and Ware agreed that good national defense included making life better for those Americans who were expected to contribute their labor and their skills to the war effort. Both women worked diligently to that end and accomplished a good deal, but in the end both resigned.

Ware did not remain out of things for long. She was part of an Office of Price Administration consumer advisory group and continued in various advisory posts until 1952, when the Eisenhower administration exhibited no concern for consumers in any form.

In 1942 she found a full-time teaching job at Howard University, a Washington institution founded in 1867 for the liberal education of freedmen and by the 1940s the preeminent site of higher education for African Americans of both sexes. She was assigned to teach constitutional history. John Hope Franklin, at the time a Howard colleague, asked to remember what she was like in those days, responded with enthusiasm: "She was bright, lively and charming! I admired her."[15] At Howard, that same year, she would meet Pauli Murray, who had heard there was an interesting teacher of constitutional law in the History Department. The friendship initiated then would last until Pauli's death in 1985.

14. Susan Ware, interview with Caroline Ware, 75–78.
15. Personal conversation, winter 2005.

Growing Up Segregated

Like Ware, Murray had a loving family to which she was devoted, and, like her, she was often the brightest kid in school—but there the similarity in their upbringings ended. Born in Baltimore, child of a nurse and a public school teacher, Murray's heritage was a mix of black and white, with—she later liked to add—perhaps some Irish and some Cherokee. Pauli was only three when her mother died. She was adopted by the schoolteacher aunt for whom she was named and taken to live with her maternal grandparents in Durham, North Carolina.

Her grandfather, Robert Fitzgerald, son of a white mother and a black father and a veteran of both the Union army and the Union navy, had come to Orange County, North Carolina, after the Civil War to teach freedpeople. Though his mixed parentage and his Union background defied all the mores of the white community, he somehow managed to establish a school, and after a few encounters, when he showed himself ready to fight back, the Ku Klux Klan left him alone. Several members of his family joined him in North Carolina, and one by one those who decided to stay moved to Durham. One brother became a prosperous brickmaker and was also among the founders of the first black-owned bank in town. Other members of the clan also climbed into the middle class. The Fitzgeralds, Murray would later write, were people who valued themselves, who stood, in the phrase she used in her family history, in "proud shoes."

Soon after he arrived in North Carolina, Robert Fitzgerald had married Cornelia Smith, whose parents were Sidney Smith, a white planter-lawyer, and a slave woman. As a child Cornelia had been virtually adopted and raised by Mary Smith, Sidney's sister, who had inherited her father's slaves. Along with four other slave children, Cornelia had been baptized in the white Chapel of the Cross in Chapel Hill. Family legend had it that her marriage had been permitted only after Mary Smith's satisfactory interview with the prospective bridegroom. As a child, Pauli often heard her grandmother Cornelia speak with pride of her father, Sidney Smith, whom she always described as one of the leading lawyers in North Carolina.

Several of Robert and Cornelia Fitzgerald's children and grandchildren were light enough in color to "pass" in white society, had they chosen to do so. None did. Pauli Murray herself would always be aware of her mixed heritage. She occupied, she wrote, "a no man's land between the whites and the blacks, belonging wholly to neither, yet irrevocably tied to both [. . .] always at the vital nerve center of racial conflict, stretched taut between strong bonds of kinship and tides of rebellion."[16]

By the time young Pauli joined the household, Robert Fitzgerald was blind. The family owned a small house and a tiny lot, along with some farm land Cornelia had inherited from Mary Smith, but was not otherwise prosperous. They made do with Robert's minuscule Civil War pension, combined with the earnings of two schoolteacher daughters.

What we know about Murray's childhood comes from the memories recorded in her autobiographies and from several interviews conducted over her adult life.

Pauli was a precocious child. At age four, taken to school by her aunt, who had no access to child care, she learned to read by listening to first graders do their lessons. By the time she was seven or eight, it was her daily task to read the newspaper to her blind grandfather.

Growing up when segregation was the law of the state, she was early aware of the vast gap between schools for white children and those to which she and her aunts were relegated. Like her aunts, she walked miles to avoid segregated streetcars, but it was not possible to avoid the "whites only" signs, the patronizing attitude with which her aunt was treated by the white school inspector, or any of the endless customary slights to which all black people were subjected.

Despite the psychic burden of discrimination, her life was far from dismal. She was good at sports and became a leader in her school. The only flaws on her report cards were low marks for "deportment"—at an early age, challenging people with whom she differed came naturally to her. One summer she won a prize for checking out the largest number of books of any patron of the "colored branch" of the Durham Public Library.

At sixteen she graduated from high school after completing eleven grades—all there were—determined to have nothing more to do with segregated schools. Under the influence of a favorite teacher she fixed her ambitions on New York City, about which she knew, literally, nothing.

16. Murray, *Song in a Weary Throat*, 390.

The teacher had worn a sweatshirt bearing the seal of Columbia University, so it was to Columbia that Pauli Murray proposed to go. One of her numerous cousins lived in Queens and offered her a place to live. Accompanied by her aunt Pauline Dame, she managed to get to New York. After, as she put it, being "jolted into reality," she enrolled in the twelfth grade at Richmond Hill High School in order to qualify for Hunter College. She was the only "colored person" among the 4,000 students in Richmond Hill.

Though teachers tried to help her make up for poor preparation, her first grades were a shock. Accustomed to being at the head of the class in Durham, she now found herself hanging on by her fingernails. Many years later she confessed that in the beginning she had harbored a secret fear that she could not compete with white students. But it was not her habit to give up on anything once undertaken, and by dint of extraordinary effort she managed to graduate with honors among the top twenty-five seniors.

In adolescence Murray had begun to worry about her sexual nature. She later said that she was probably meant to be a man, but had by accident turned up in a woman's body. She began to keep clippings about various experiments with hormones as a way of changing sexual identity. In 1937 her friend Adelene MacBean would commit her to Bellvue Hospital in New York for "observation and evaluation." In her usual systematic way, while there Pauli wrote an analysis of her own personality and talked at length with a psychiatrist about her concerns.

Such worries did not slow her down; if anything, they had the opposite effect. After a year back in Durham typing for a local black-owned business to earn money, she enrolled in a branch of Hunter College in New York City. Not for the first time and certainly not for the last, when faced with a daunting challenge, she demonstrated a great capacity for hard work. At Hunter she replaced "colored" with "Negro" in referring to people like herself. Later, when people all around her shifted to "African American" or "black," she stuck to "Negro."

Even at this early stage a characteristic that would shape her life was evident. Something about her attracted many people, white and black, male and female, and very often inspired them to help her. The women she met at Barnard College (to which she had turned when she discovered that Columbia was for men only) instead of simply telling her she was not educationally qualified, and certainly could not afford the tuition, went to some trouble to help her find a way to prepare for a tuition-free college. Several of her high school and college teachers went out of their way for her. As the letters in this book show, Caroline Ware, from the beginning of their friendship, was endlessly helpful, as was Eleanor Roosevelt, who was supportive even when she thought Murray unreasonable.

Though she often described herself as shy, Murray did not hesitate to approach anyone whose work she admired or whose help she wanted. Her friendship with Stephen Vincent Benét is a case in point. Seeing herself as an apprentice writer who needed guidance and having found *John Brown's Body* inspiring, in 1939 she wrote Benét a fan letter telling him that his example had encouraged her to try her hand at a long poem, that she had no way of obtaining useful criticism, and asked for an interview. He answered warmly but took the precaution of asking for samples of her work; she immediately posted off ten poems, which led to an invitation to visit. Benét and his wife took to her, and from that time until his death four years later he acted as a mentor and adviser who offered constant encouragement. He read and commented on her work and sent pages of wise guidance for a beginning writer. He stressed over and over his belief that learning to write was a lifetime proposition. He urged her to make her reader "see, feel, taste and smell" and much else. She gave him credit for urging her to finish *Dark Testament* and to begin the family history that became *Proud Shoes*. After his death, his wife, Rosemary, continued to be her friend.

Then there was Lloyd Garrison, grandson of nineteenth-century abolitionist leader William Lloyd Garrison, one of New York's leading lawyers, former dean of the University of Wisconsin Law School, and a member of the National War Labor Board. Organizing a dinner at Howard for students and faculty, Murray invited him to speak and, as his hostess, sat next to him during the meal. From that day, he became one of her strongest and most reliable advocates.

The salutations in her letter files read like a who's who of the twentieth century: "Dear Adlai," "Dear Thurgood," "Dear Ralph" [Bunche], "Dear Dean Hastie," "Dear Mrs. Roosevelt," and so on.

So it would be for the rest of her life. People of many kinds responded to her with great warmth. In 2004 a professor at the University of Michigan Law School who had been a young law student when Murray turned up at Yale in the 1960s still remembered her charm and spoke of her warmth, the "twinkle in her eye," and especially her helpfulness when his wife was dying. A woman who also knew her during the 1960s said she was "the most approachable public person I have ever known." These are only a few of many examples.[17]

But most of this was yet to come when she entered Hunter College in 1928 at age eighteen. For two years she managed to keep herself afloat financially with a dizzying array of jobs and make-do arrangements. Then came the time when there seemed to be no jobs of any kind. Life in New York for a young black woman from the South had been difficult enough, even before the 1929 crash left the city with a large body of unemployed. Now it seemed close to impossible. At the end of her sophomore year she could no longer pay Hunter's modest fees. In the autobiography published after her death she described the ups and downs of her life in the Depression, a description mostly borne out by the contemporary record in her papers. These included a brief and disastrous marriage; a hitchhiking, work-for-food-as-we-go trip with a friend around the Midwest; riding the rails across country dressed as a boy after a futile attempt to find work in California; and several periods when she verged on starvation. The years from 1929 to 1936, even when she was able to return to Hunter, or to find work, were extremely difficult. She would come to think that the bad health that dogged her adult life was partly the result of malnutrition in her youth. The contrast with Caroline Ware's Depression experience could hardly have been greater. Nevertheless, so all-pervasive was the New Deal that it affected Pauli too.

By 1931 Murray was able to return to Hunter, from which she graduated two years later, one of five African Americans in her class of 232. She worked for a while at the National Urban League, then—on doctor's orders—gave up that job and went to Camp Tera, a New Deal work project for women in rural New York similar to the Civilian Conservation Corps, which had been Hilda Smith's idea. Murray's health im-

17. Layman Allen, professor of law at the University of Michigan, and Ruth Emerson, widow of Professor Tom Emerson, who had been a major influence on Pauli's legal training at Yale.

proved dramatically, and it was at Camp Tera that she first encountered Eleanor Roosevelt, who would become the guiding heroine of her life. After clashing with the camp's program director, who had been outraged to find a copy of *Das Kapital* in her room, Pauli left and found work with a WPA reading program and with the Urban League's magazine, *Opportunity*.

In 1938 she decided to combine responsibility to her Durham aunts (who very much wanted her to come home) with further education, and so she applied for admission to graduate work in sociology at the University of North Carolina, saying she wanted to study the problems of race with Guy Johnson and Howard Odum, who were making a name for themselves in that field. Frank Porter Graham, who was then president of the university, left to himself, would probably have admitted her, but state law and the glowering presence of the state legislature tied his hands (see Appendix). Once her application became public, the white undergraduates erupted in protest and, in total ignorance of who she was, some called her many ugly names and made dire threats of what they would do, should she be admitted. The graduate students, by contrast, in an informal poll, voted two to one to admit her. Meantime the local and national press had a field day.

In this case, as in so many yet to come, Pauli Murray did not accept defeat easily. She tried to enlist the National Association for the Advancement of Colored People (NAACP) on her side, citing the recent *Gaines* decision in which the Supreme Court had decided that the refusal of the state of Missouri to admit a black citizen to its only state-supported law school was unconstitutional. The NAACP lawyers pointed out that her years in New York meant that, unlike Gaines, Murray was not clearly a resident of the state from which she was demanding a right to an advanced education. Despite this caution, and foreshadowing her later comment that one woman with a typewriter made a movement, she wrote a number of well-argued and compelling letters to the university and sent copies to area newspapers. But to no avail.

In the midst of her unhappy experience with the University of North Carolina, that institution conferred an honorary degree on President Roosevelt, who, in accepting, spoke of UNC as "a great liberal institution." This was too much for Murray, who wrote a bitter letter confronting FDR with his inaction on the race question and denouncing his description of the university that had turned its back on her. The letter typified her forthright style:

> 12,000,000 of your citizens have to endure insults, injustices, and such degradation of the spirit as you would believe impossible [. . .] the un-Christian, un-American conditions in the South, make it impossible for me and other young Negroes to live there and continue our faith in the ideals of democracy and Christianity. We are as much political refugees from the South as any of the Jews in Germany. We cannot endure these conditions [. . .].[18]

She went on to argue that the ultimate test for the United States was its commitment to solving what she and many others called its "Negro problem." To make sure the president saw her letter, she sent a copy to Mrs. Roosevelt, who replied that she understood but that great change must come slowly. Thus began a correspondence between Murray and Eleanor Roosevelt that lasted until the latter's death.

In 1940 came what forever after Murray would call "the bus incident." She and a friend were traveling on a Greyhound bus through Virginia on the way to North Carolina when the two women found the back seat, to which they had gone, broken and uncomfortable, especially for Pauli's friend, who was recovering from an operation. The women asked permission to move forward where there were vacant seats in the part of the bus reserved for white people. The driver brusquely told them to go back where they belonged. Tension rose, the police were called, and in the end the two women were arrested for "disturbing the peace" and sent to jail in Petersburg, Virginia. They had recently been studying Gandhian non-violence and decided to practice on the jailer (who had been most unfriendly) as well as on the male inmates who jeered them. A very polite letter asked the jailer for the supplies promised in the posted rules—clean sheets, towels, and soap, and the belongings taken from them when they were booked. As for the male inmates, who had jeered and harassed the women, Murray later wrote: "We composed a polite memorandum giving a brief account of our arrest and stressing the injustice of racial segregation. When we slipped it under the door the effect was surprising.

18. Murray, *Song in a Weary Throat*, 111–12.

The jeering comments gradually ceased as the memorandum circulated [. . .]."[19] She had managed to get word of their arrest to the NAACP, which sent a lawyer to defend them. They were, predictably, found guilty, and their lawyer gave notice of appeal. The case played itself out, as did many others in those years, in a way that disappointed the women's hopes that it might ultimately be the basis for an appeal to the Supreme Court, which might dispose of the constitutionality of segregation.

In August of 1942 Murray again wrote an angry letter to the president by way of Mrs. Roosevelt. This time the reply from Eleanor Roosevelt was stern: addressed to "Dear Miss Murray," the six-paragraph letter, in effect, told Pauli that she understood very little of the realities of a president's life and included the sentence, "For one who must really have a knowledge of the workings of our kind of government, your letter seems to me one of the most thoughtless I have ever read."[20]

Nothing daunted, Murray responded with an apology for intemperate words but reiterated her earlier argument that, if black people were to fight in a war devoted to freedom, then there must be leadership from the top to free them from discrimination at home. At this point Mrs. Roosevelt invited her to the White House, greeted her—literally—with open arms, and they continued the discussion. Their friendship continued to develop. When Murray graduated from law school in 1944, a huge bouquet from the White House attracted considerable attention.

Murray was deeply involved in the case of Odell Waller, a black southern sharecropper who shot his white landlord when the latter refused to live up to the agreement between them. Waller claimed that he feared for his life, thinking the landlord was drawing a gun. Pauli and many others believed that he had been cheated because he was black and threatened when he talked back. Working with the Workers Defense League, she poured enormous energy and emotion into the cause and again called on her burgeoning friendship with Eleanor Roosevelt, who, in turn, urged clemency on the governor of Virginia. Despite all efforts, Waller was found guilty of first-degree murder and executed.

No matter how often Eleanor Roosevelt perceived Pauli as hotheaded

19. Ibid., 145.

20. Eleanor Roosevelt to Pauli Murray, August 3, 1942, Pauli Murray File, Eleanor Roosevelt Papers, Franklin D. Roosevelt Library, Hyde Park, N.Y.

and naive, she remained a steadfast friend. There are dozens of letters to Murray in the Roosevelt Papers. Some invited her to the White House, others to Val Kill at Hyde Park or to lunch at the United Nations. Pauli eventually took every member of her family (one or two at a time) to visit Mrs. R, as she called her. The warmth and generosity of Eleanor Roosevelt's responses continued throughout her life. When she died in 1962, Pauli fantasized that she could feel Roosevelt's influence from beyond the grave. In a note to Joseph Lash when he was writing *Eleanor and Franklin*, Murray wrote: "I suspect that I was one of the rarely privileged people to do battle toe-to-toe with her in the earlier stages of our friendship and to emerge with a bond so deep that it had a psychic and mystical quality." She went on to say that she felt Mrs. R's spirit being troubled by what was going on in the world and that she felt appointed to carry on Eleanor Roosevelt's work.[21]

After the University of North Carolina turned her down, and after she failed to save Odell Waller, Pauli again debated her future. She had long seen herself as, above all, a writer, and she was indeed writing poetry and some prose. But there was not much hope that she could earn a living writing. She met Leon Ransom, a member of the Howard Law School faculty who, like so many others, recognized her abilities. He not only advised her to study law, but also arranged a scholarship to make it possible. In later years she would at times point to the Waller case as having decided her future direction. At other times she would say that her ambition to be a lawyer had begun early, when her grandmother spoke so glowingly of Pauli's great-grandfather as "one of North Carolina's great lawyers."

Once in law school, Murray began organizing Howard students to oppose segregation in the District of Columbia and to practice nonviolence by sitting-in at two restaurants in the neighborhood of the university, both of which were eventually integrated. Emboldened, the students tried again, this time in a restaurant on Pennsylvania Avenue, where they were temporarily successful, but the university administrators, who feared congressional retaliation in the form of budget cuts, persuaded them to desist.

21. Pauli Murray Folder, Joseph Lash Papers, Franklin D. Roosevelt Library, Hyde Park, N.Y.

At Howard there was, of course, no discrimination on grounds of race—but sex was another matter. As the only woman in her class, Murray found herself constantly excluded from the profession-related activities open to male students. She began to realize that discrimination was not solely a matter of color. It was this exclusion, she said, that led to her determination to graduate at the top of her class.

In her second year at Howard she met Lina Ware. For the next forty years their lives would be entwined. What allowed these two women, from such totally different backgrounds, to become lifelong friends and collaborators?

In spite of their great differences in early experience and in style, they shared a good many characteristics. Both were gifted with high intelligence. (Meeting a niece of Ware's, Murray exclaimed: "We [meaning herself and the niece] share the finest mind in America!") Each was way ahead of most people in her field, and their interests often converged. In order to write *Proud Shoes*, Murray made herself into a first-rate social historian; both were interested in constitutional law and shared a passion for human rights. Murray's enthusiastic words in an early letter, "I'm proud as punch of you and me" expressed her feeling that they were partners in a major cause: to bridge the gap between white and black. Both read a great deal and wrote and talked well.

Each was known for her remarkable capacity for hard, sustained, work. Both loved teaching and liked to talk about its rewards and pitfalls. Each had a loving family for whom she felt considerable responsibility.

Each also had a large network of friends, with some overlap. Perhaps the most notable was in their shared admiration for Eleanor Roosevelt. Murray said that Roosevelt "filled the . . . landscape of my adult life,"[22] and Ware not only thought she "towered over all the others" but also took it upon herself to remind every gathering of old New Dealers that Eleanor was as important in her way as Franklin was in his.[23]

22. Murray, *Song in a Weary Throat*, 351: "She had filled the landscape of my entire adult life as she had for millions of my generation, and it was unthinkable to associate her with death."

23. Susan Ware, interview with Caroline Ware. Lina spoke often about her admiration for Mrs. Roosevelt. For one of many examples, see her letter of February 1, 1972, below, where she observes, on reading *Eleanor and Franklin*, "how much more

Each had many relationships, many friends, and many activities in which the other was not involved. Occasionally a year would pass without much written communication between them. At other times one or the other wrote every few days for a while. As long as Pauli lived (for, though the younger of the two, she died first) they were constantly in touch, by mail, phone, and visits.

These surviving letters take the reader back to what now seems not only an earlier but a simpler time. They paint a picture of the development of a most unusual friendship and throw light on some of the major issues of the middle decades of the twentieth century, particularly those touching on questions of racial discrimination and civil rights.

As time went by both Murray and Ware became increasingly involved with issues surrounding the status of women. There, too, the theme was equality of opportunity and "the revolution of rising participation," the phrase Ware used to characterize her lifework. It was an exciting journey.

------

incredible Mrs. R becomes as a person, the more one knows." Lina said that whenever old New Dealers gathered and talked about Franklin, she stood up and said, "We must not forget about Eleanor."

✦ 1

THE

CORRESPONDENCE

BEGINS

In 1942 the country was at war, and victory was by no means certain. War production was barely under way, though President Roosevelt assured citizens that they could do what was necessary. They could indeed, and in a very short time the needs of the war would take over the economy, with attendant disruptions to the accustomed way of doing things. For black citizens, war brought opportunities for work in defense plants or in service jobs hitherto filled by white people. It also brought army service and overseas experience to many young black men. These changes would bear directly on the concern for human rights shared by Pauli Murray and Caroline Ware.

It was in this wartime context that the two became friends. Ware was forty-two, Murray ten years younger. They began with something of a teacher-student relationship. In the ensuing year the two met often, in class and out, and became well acquainted. Murray drew Ware into the student protest movement she had helped to organize seeking to end segregation in Washington, D.C. Ware introduced Murray to The Farm and to Gardiner, of whom Murray soon spoke as a friend.

The two women responded in various ways to the events of the 1940s. Ware served on the National Defense Advisory Commission, wrote *The Consumer Goes to War*, worked in her garden, and taught history to soldiers-in-the-making. Murray, whose focus was on the struggle for human rights, was engaged in active protest and in the study of law. She argued vehemently in many venues that the United States could not claim to be fighting for freedom as long as it permitted discrimination against black citizens. Whatever the two women may have discussed or thought in other settings, their letters exhibit no interest in the military situation that filled the headlines.

In the summer of 1943, at the end of her second year in law school,

Murray went off to New York to earn a little money during the summer vacation, and the correspondence began.

Like most professional women of her generation, Lina Ware was deeply involved in the work of several voluntary associations. The American Association of University Women was her longest-running volunteer base.[1] Within that organization she supported racial integration long before the membership as a whole was ready for such a change. She promoted the idea of consumer protection within the organization as well and often represented the AAUW before congressional committees and various governmental bodies.

Planting potatoes and corn was, possibly, a response to wartime need; however, a large vegetable garden continued for many years to be characteristic of the Ware-Means ménage, and Lina Ware always found that gardening restored her after hard work in other dimensions of her life.

Vassar, of which she was a loyal alumna and former faculty member, was one of her frequent ports of call. She often went to spend time with her close friend of many years, Helen Lockwood, a member of the English Department, with whom she shared a deep interest in what was going on at the college. Next to Gardiner Means, Lockwood was her closest intellectual companion.

→ Vienna, Virginia
14 July 1943
Dear Pauli:
[The letter begins with advice about training a Sheltie puppy given Pauli by the Ware-Means family.] I have a reprieve on teaching for which I am thoroughly glad. The summer school enrollment is so small that I had no classes. That let me replant corn, and finish the potatoes last week. Then, when I called to find my schedule for army classes, I managed to

---

1. The AAUW began in 1881 as the Association of Collegiate Alumnae, at a time when fewer than 2 percent of all college graduates were women, with the purpose of expanding opportunities for women scholars. In 1921 the name was changed to the present one, and by 1940 more than 12 percent of all American women were college graduates. See the excellent book by Susan Levine, *Degrees of Equality: The American Association of University Women and the Challenge of Twentieth-Century Feminism* (Philadelphia: Temple University Press, 1995).

arrange not to start with the first batch of boys who came in today but to start with the batch that comes in the middle of July. So I can go to Vassar for a couple of weeks and farm for the rest of June—with time out for an AAUW board meeting in the midst of which I am now—one week on the farm has almost put me back into circulation.

A little more and I will be 100%. [The rest of the letter is about friends and dogs.]

Be good—Pumpkin—Lina

Two weeks later Murray responds on the letterhead of the Workers Defense League, an organization with which she had worked on the Odell Waller case, and one that the FBI and the House Committee on Un-American Activities considered to be Communist controlled. Common Sense was a progressive journal for which she had written a number of essays. She was also writing for the newspaper PM and other contemporary publications. Her "first long poem" was Dark Testament. Her comment that "you will hardly recognize" the Common Sense article suggests that she had already begun what would become her lifelong habit of sending drafts to her mentor for editing and comment. The misspelling "Lena" suggests that this was an early letter; the error did not occur again.

⤷ July 31, 1943
Dear Lena,

Have just finished typing my first long poem. It represents six years of struggling with words. I've put my best into it. What more can I say. Either you'll say I'm a poet when you finish this—or you'll tell me to study law and leave the poetry be.

Incidentally, may I take you up on that offer to coach me in Constitutional Law? If so where will you be Sept. 1–13?

I'm "slinging hash"—better known as waiting table down town at Allerton House Grill on east 39th street. Doing pretty well. Getting plenty of fruit juices and nourishing foods, and leaving some time free to whip my writing into shape. The Common Sense article was slashed so, you'll hardly recognize it at all. It's less than one-fourth its original length, hence jumpy and says little. Be good—Pauli

[A handwritten note at the top of the page adds:] I joined the Socialist

Party about two weeks ago. FDR is unhappily wedded to white supremacy, I am afraid.

During Pauli Murray's final year at Howard the two women were once again in the same place, and there is no record of what they talked about. Murray was still involved in the ongoing student protests against segregation in the District of Columbia, and was, at the same time, studying ferociously hard. Ware, while teaching, continued to be in and out of the government as a consultant on consumer matters.

When Murray succeeded in graduating at the head of her class and as a result was given the Rosenwald Scholarship for advanced work in law, she followed a long-standing Howard tradition by applying to Harvard Law School for graduate work. The dean responded frostily, "Your picture and the salutation on your college transcript indicate that you are not of the sex entitled to be admitted to the Harvard Law School." She protested in several forceful letters, but despite strong support for her application from President Roosevelt and other weighty alumni, Harvard did not relent.[2] Now, in the summer of 1944, she is in California, planning to enter Boalt Hall, the Law School at the University of California at Berkeley, as soon as there is a place for her. While she waits, she is earning her living as a journalist, sending articles to PM and other left-wing publications.[3] One theme runs through all the early letters— whatever else she is doing, Pauli Murray sees herself as a writer needing time to practice her craft.

Ware writes from a summer institute at Vassar; as usual she has her finger in several pies at once. Teaching at a summer school for office workers is part of her lifelong commitment to helping people who wanted more education.

2. Pauli Murray, *Song in a Weary Throat: An American Pilgrimage* (New York: Harper and Row, 1987), 239.

3. *PM* was a lively radical tabloid that, during its short life (1940–48), was a leader in journalistic innovation. See Paul Milkman, *PM: A New Deal in Journalism, 1940–1948* (New Brunswick, N.J.: Rutgers University Press, 1997).

→ Vassar Summer Institute
Poughkeepsie, N.Y.
August 8 [1944]
Hi Little Lamb P

I was glad to hear that you had got to L.A. I want to hear more of what you are finding and doing. Mrs. R.[4] was here, & mentioned, when I tried to bring her up to date on your whereabouts, that she had heard from you—and that it would be easier to keep up with you if you weren't such a bobber-upper (language mine not hers).

My summer has been spotty—a good YW[CA] national conference, a bat at summer school for office workers. Then 3 weeks at the Vassar Summer Institute. Pauline [Coggs, who worked for the Washington Urban League] came up here to give an excellent lecture on housing. Then we had a race relations forum which blew the lid off & has caused revelations a-plenty [from] Jewish, Negro, Chinese & white gentile Americans. The group was shocked to hear what the Negro women tend to think of whites. Ever since they have been trying to get me to tell them it wasn't true—

Now I am off for a week with my parents in New England. Then back to Washington and job hunting. I haven't yet decided just how & where. I miss the kids at Howard. I enclose a messy copy of a poem I came across the other day and thought you would like. Do I gather that you are doing some writing? And are you working for Mr. McBetty? And are you headed for Berkeley? And have you had yourself a bit of rest and added flesh to those bones? I hope so. Whatever it is, good luck and affectionate greetings—Skipper

Two days later Murray writes this odd letter that sounds more like one from a college freshman than from a young woman of thirty-four. Her casual style includes giving up capital letters as well as using slang words and many ellipses. She complains that Lina Ware has not written her recently. "Al" and "Pauline" are not identified, but presumably are people who share her antisegregation activism. The story of her hair-raising trip to California with her sister Mildred, a nurse, is found also in Song

4. Mrs. R is Eleanor Roosevelt, with whom Pauli had established a friendship.

in a Weary Throat. *The tone and the use of lowercase does not continue in future letters.*

→¦ "The Barn" 5871 Crocker St. (no crockers have appeared yet)
L.A.3, Cal.
August 10, 1944
Well, Skipper, you're trying to see if I can take it huh? You won't write, huh? Just for that am sending progress report of the doings of Pauli Frantic and the musings of Peter Panic. So there.

May I celebrate the occasion of receipt of a check for $100.00 for *Dark Testament*, sold to *South Today*,[5] and $50.00 check from P.M. for a revised Footnote for Minority Americans. The story of the P.M. check is a scream. While on the way two tires blew out, our money was low, I wired P.M. from Pittsfield, Ill., saying funds depleted, special story on the way, wire advance and Harold Lavine, assistant editor out of the goodness of his heart wired personal loan of $50.00 ahead to Denver. The $50 bought two new tires, tools and car repairs so was broke again upon arrival. I borrowed $100 dollars to eat while typing and revising Dark Testament, and now the 100 of Lillian Smith repays that loan and I'm broke again, but writing for a living.

Covered the FEPC[6] Los Angeles Railway story for PM. Wired them a story on blind instinct collect, using PM check to cover costs of wire until

5. *The South Today* was a journal published by Lillian Smith and Paula Snelling in Georgia. Smith had written novels and many articles in which she criticized the South's racial patterns. Murray had written her a fan letter, and a correspondence ensued. Later Smith would offer help when Murray was writing *Proud Shoes*, but she was first very busy and later ill, so the correspondence faded. Smith published *Dark Testament* and also commissioned an autobiographical piece for her journal.

6. On June 25, 1941, President Roosevelt had created the Fair Employment Practices Committee (FEPC) by executive order. The order forbade discrimination on the basis of race, creed, color, or national origin in the employment of workers in any industry receiving government contracts. A. Philip Randolph and several others had threatened to lead a march on Washington unless the president took some such action. When industry failed to comply, FDR increased the FEPC's budget and strengthened its enforcement powers. By the end of World War II, the proportion of African Americans in the nation's factories had reached an all-time high.

it was rejected or accepted, then when the news got hotter, on sheer chance wired another long story, then scooped the settlement between fepc employers and union last night, first reporter hit wires with union settlement and statement from fepc, only to find later that harold lavine had wired the day before to send 1,000 word story on the situation. Is that mental telepathy or aint it.

Al will get a laugh out of this one. Tell him I'm a lousy little reporter on an up and coming little Negro paper called the Los Angeles Sentinel, and one of my superiors on paper is Loren Miller, the managing editor is J. Robert Smith, formerly of Amsterdam News Afro, Public Relations for United Seaman's organization, on west coast for about two years, one of the organizers of National Negro Congress in Philadelphia and former organizer in American Youth Congress. How'm I doing for walking into lion's den? The story is already around town that I am a trotskyite, and dear brother Smith killed a feature story of mine on interview with six L.A. railway workers which according to publisher was *the* story of the week, and now publisher is sore with smith because he assigned me to do it, and the office is in uproar in less than three days. Oh well, it's nice to know that there are worse things than messing up on an exam—having your story killed for instance after you risked your neck to talk to guys and gals that spewed out venom stronger than lye, and some that didn't.

Reynal and Hitchcock's editor-in-chief, Frank E. Taylor, writes me at Howard asking how about an interview—and me 3200 miles away from dream of a lifetime. My "agent" Clara Clayman is seeing him in New York for me. Shall it be a novel, Skipper or a Master's in law? I am considering each, maybe both.

Harvard has still not recovered from a letter which ended thusly: "Humorously, gentlemen, I'd happily change my sex to fulfill your requirements but since the way has not been revealed as to how I can do this, there is no other recourse but to induce you to change your minds." One smart alecy friend said I should have used another word, but that Harvard is wise—it would never be the same if they break down and let me in. But a local legal sheet reports and Dean Hastie affirms there is every likelihood they [Harvard] will open the Medical School to women in 1945.[7]

7. William Henry Hastie (1904–76), a native of Tennessee, had graduated from Amherst College and Harvard Law School. He had advised the Roosevelt administra-

Judge Sarah Hughes writes from Texas, July 31, "this is not a matter [her rejection by Harvard] that the Committee on Economic and Legal status of Women of the American Association etc [of University Women] has considered. However, I shall be glad to discuss the problem at the next meeting of the committee which is in September [...]. If there is any change in your situation, will you please advise me. After the meeting of the Committee I will write you with reference to its attitude."

Hopeful enough, I'd say. You can snoop around if you like.

With a letter from the Surgeon General's office Army reaffirming "jimcrow" blood donor policy, while admitting my statement with reference to no scientific distinction in human blood is in accord with the belief of such office due to protest after I was personally solicited for blood here and told no segregation then later told Negro blood was separated because Negro soldiers had asked for Negro blood—praise peanuts —that about ends the story of the mad-murray-go-round enterprises.

Oh yes—university of california says maybe with juggling of schedules and modifications of certain courses I submitted it can take me in October 1944. Original information after arriving here was it couldn't take me until march 1945 when Mrs. Armstrong, labor law specialist returns.[8]

NOW SKIPPER—what's wrong? Are you canning, fighting drought,

---

tion on race relations and, appointed by FDR, was the first African American federal judge. He was dean of the Howard Law School and then a civilian aide to the secretary of defense until he resigned in 1943 to protest discrimination in the armed forces. Later he was governor of the Virgin Islands and then a judge on the Federal District Court of the Virgin Islands. He worked with Charles Houston and Thurgood Marshall in preparing for *Brown v. Board of Education*. Murray, who said he had been a major influence in her life, thought he should have been on the Supreme Court.

Harvard finally voted to admit women to the Medical School in June of 1944 after a long discussion and some "scenes of disorder and confusion at the Faculty meetings" (Joint Committee on the Status of Women of Harvard Medical School, "Matriculation of Women, 1921–1947").

8. Barbara Nachtrieb Armstrong (1909–76) was a highly regarded specialist in economics and law who had been much engaged in public policy both on the state level in California and on the federal level. See Susan Ware, ed., *Notable American Women: A Biographical Dictionary Completing the Twentieth Century* (Cambridge: Harvard University Press, 2004), 28–29.

teaching at vassar, taking a vacation, going back to howard or not going back to howard next fall—or what?

Am I entitled to know anything or am i really in doghouse exile or what. al won't answer a letter, pauline won't answer, you wont answer, the matter of restaurants looks as if the commies have moved in if washington tribune is accurate—is that good bad or indifferent—and is the east as decadent as some people here would have me believe? love to all—pauli.

P.s. west wind blowing by peter panic—flash . . . flash sister mil becomes first sepia nurse at federal veterans hospital bonsall in west los angeles next door to beautiful beverly hills . . . sidelights of fepc hearings . . . mike rose looks like harpo marx and seems quite nice on surface . . . realized I was covering for pm so gave me the breaks on the news . . . boris shishkin drew sketches of the witnesses all during the hearing . . . so cute i sent 'em in to pm. to let them know labor has other talents too . . . houston[9] made the pale americans sit up and take notice . . . one white spectator said to me who's that fellow on the end . . . he's sharp as a tack . . . sure i answered he ought to be on the supreme court bench . . . harris, president of lary (los angeles railway co.) looked like a wet mouse all during the hearing, didn't dare say a word without his lawyer, but during negotiations with fepc and union yesterday looked like man who has got religion—we talked happily about time when l.a. will have super express highways, cut in subways, express busses, and get rid of his ole street cars entirely. can you beat that . . . I told him what lousy service the cars had now . . . i had to wait 15 or 20 minutes waiting for a car, then got disgusted and walked . . . and he said . . . and we lose a fare . . . they're all human those old geezers. . . .

As a newspaper reporter seeking a telephone interview, Pauli Murray manages to connect with U.S. Supreme Court Justice Frank Murphy. Her approach to him is a good example of the way she introduces herself to people she wants to know.

9. Charles Houston (1895–1950), one of the outstanding lawyers of his generation, the first black editor of the *Harvard Law Review*, and a special counsel to the NAACP, was involved in many of the landmark cases of the early civil rights movement. See Genna Rae McNeil, *Groundwork: Charles Houston and the Struggle for Civil Rights* (Philadelphia: University of Pennsylvania Press, 1983).

She offers Murphy her strong belief that segregation is inherently unconstitutional—that "separate but equal" will not do. At Howard she had written a long paper based on the argument that, since color cannot be changed, it cannot be the basis for a permanent limitation. Her argument, seen as too extreme by her professor in law school, appears in the Brown case, and years later she learned that Thurgood Marshall had had access to her paper. She liked to believe that Marshall had picked up her idea.

As she writes this letter, the Allied armies are moving across France and Paris has been liberated. Possibly she and Ware had talked about this development, but her letters tend to reflect what she herself described as her preoccupation with the issue of racial justice. When she writes elsewhere about the war, it is to reiterate her point that black people in a segregated society can hardly be expected to fight for freedom.

Already, after two years acquaintance she speaks of herself as a "product" of Professor Ware's teaching, though she had plenty of ideas of her own. She asserts that they are on a joint crusade to bridge the racial divide.

⤷ September 16, 1944

Dear Skipper:

Not being one to "pout" when you don't write, I'm reporting two encouraging pieces of information on the two-man battle to decrease "social distance" being conducted by Major Ware and Pup-Private Murray:

As you will see by the *Sentinel*, the little lamb had an interview with Associate Justice Frank Murphy.[10] Don't mind telling you I have been opportunist enough to use my press card to get these interviews, and my legal training—non-lawyer status to talk law with these "big guys." Have learned that not being any more than a law student and a gal, you can completely disarm them and get more information than the FBI. Well,

10. Frank Murphy (1890–1949), who began life as a child worker in a factory, wound up on the Supreme Court, appointed by FDR. Before his appointment, he had been mayor of Detroit, governor of Michigan, and attorney general of the United States. On the Court he had a record of firm support of civil rights. See Sidney Fine, *Frank Murphy*, 2 vols. (Vol. 1, Ann Arbor: University of Michigan Press, 1975; Vol. 2, Chicago: University of Chicago Press, 1984).

anyway, this was telephonic conversation with the Associate Justice. After getting the statement for the *Sentinel*, I asked his opinion on the question of bringing up these bases to overrule precedents like the *Civil Rights Cases* and *Plessy v. Ferguson* based upon straight reasoning and not attempting to get around the various interpretations of the 14th Amendment later built up. I told him there was a trend of thinking among the younger law students to strike straight at the heart of segregation, but that older lawyers were afraid of unfavorable decisions in view of further fixing the law.

He replied, "There never was a better chance to get a review of these cases in the 160 years of the Court, and I want to encourage you to stick to your point of view. Justice is the thing you want to hammer at—don't mind the precedents." He told me furthermore, he'd be glad to give me more time to discuss this personally, if I'd call his secretary and make the appointment. He'll be here several days longer, and I'm still wangling for that appointment and an autograph. Got Biddle's,[11] of course.

Now Skipper, how's that for (a) major strategy? (b) carrying the lobbying idea straight to the S. Ct. Who knows? Maybe five years from now I'll be arguing Plessy v. Ferguson before the old boys up there, and might just as well find out how they feel before I'm barred from informal questions as a member of the bar. I cannot tell you how this conversation encouraged me. Have you been watching Murphy's dissents? Also he wrote the decision in Hartzel v. U.S., the case Billy Jones and I heard argued before the Court, and the one in which the Court by a five-to-four decision refused to apply the Espionage Acts to some very "nasty" writing one Hartzel did about the President etc. See National Bar Journal, September 1944 for review of same.

Furthermore, Honorable Mr. Murphy said "You can guess what my view will be when such a case gets up there." I asked him what he thought of the idea that "an arbitrary classification by color was unconstitutional and not within the police power of the state," pointing out that with other classifications, by change of status or circumstances one could remove

11. Francis Biddle (1886–1968) was a member of a prominent Philadelphia family and a graduate of Harvard Law School. At the time this letter was written, he was attorney general of the United States and a trusted member of the New Deal inner circle. After World War II he was a U.S. judge at the Nuremberg Trials.

himself from the classification affected, but that color was fixed and thus arbitrary. He said, "You're perfectly right!"

Now Skipper, it so happens that a very dear friend of Justice Murphy's is also a large advertiser with the *Sentinel* and the advertiser said Murphy had already seen my interview with him in the paper, and that he was very much impressed with me and sorry he could not give me more time.[12] That he had noted the facts of racial tension, my story of Oxley's report, and that he would be glad to do anything he could—including a talk with [Earl] Warren, governor of the State, if we'd give him some recommendations. It's small world, aint it?

I'm proud as punch of you and me. Whose product am I anyway? Yours, or the law school's? I think it breaks even. What I'm trying to say is that I think we're on the right track, with this argument we cooked up last spring? Don't argue—I'd never had the courage to advance it if you hadn't held my hand all down the line. Carey McWilliams has written an article called "A Lawyer's View of Segregation" and I have the manuscript. His thinking and ours on the Civil Rights Acts and P.v.F. are almost identical. He gives hell to the sociologists and anthropologists who say you can't legislate away discrimination by pointing to the NLRB [National Labor Relations Board.] etc.etc., and also points out the anti-oriental laws here on the West Coast did not come about as a result of crystallization of public opinion but that public opinion was manufactured by certain interest groups who wished to profit by it—unfortunately one of them was the growing labor movement on West Coast being manipulated by politicians. I don't dare send you this manuscript, although I'm dying to, because you've been so "shut-mouf" about the others. But this article is appearing in some magazine so keep open an eye for it.

I see the Negro press still rates you as Prof. of History, Howard University, and that the good Trinity-ites are kicking at the Negro registration at American University. Who's riding the flag-pole, the American Eagle, or Jim Crow? Are you going to be at Howard this year? This question is important. Please answer. Know you're busy but think of your own lonely

---

12. A file of Murray's articles in the *Sentinel* is preserved in her papers at the Schlesinger Library. They were numerous, well written, and carefully researched. Apparently Murray had a reputation for fairness, even among those who disagreed with her.

hours at Oxford, and get a little picture of me. I was thinking maybe the hurricane would blow hard enough to blow me somebody out here for company, but nothing has fallen out of the skies yet. Ah, woe is me!

I've got a copy of the CED's [Committee on Economic Development] "Postwar Federal Tax Plan for High Employment," but must confess can't make heads or tails of it yet. I need both you and Gardiner to straighten me out.

Love to all, including puppies, kittens and baby. L-o-n-e-l-y L'll Lamb.

By 1945 Murray is in law school in Berkeley and living in International House. It is an exciting time: the war in Europe is winding down, and plans for the international conference in San Francisco to set up the United Nations are under way. Change is in the air. Of course she could not know that two weeks later President Roosevelt would die and for a little while the country, and a good part of the world, would be in shock. But on this date Pauli has found an environment that suits her very well, and her letter is unusually exuberant. (I was twenty-four that spring, and my job required writing daily about the United Nations. I remember similar enthusiasm among my contemporaries about the promise of the future. We had persuaded ourselves that many people had learned from the war that changes must be made if we were to have a better world.)

Nineteen years before the word "sex" would be included in Lyndon Johnson's Civil Rights Act of 1964 (at least partly due to Murray's efforts), Pauli is already suggesting that discrimination against women be part of a bill to establish a permanent Fair Employment Practices Committee. Despite strong support on the part of some members of Congress and many black activists, the FEPC never became permanent.

International House
Berkeley, 4, California
March 30, 1945
(Good Friday)
Dear Skipper:
Spring in California is like an idyll one reads of—roses and wisteria in late January, red rhododendron in February and soft May nights in March. Robins and blue jays all year round so far as I can see.

I've been walking on air for days now—altho there aren't enough hours to go around—there's so much to do. To begin with, the school work is fascinating because they're letting me spend my time in the research I really want to do. Have only one formal class and the rest is personal seminar of one. With Mrs. Armstrong I've galloped through all the Labor Relations Reporters since 1936, and am getting a bird's eye view on the evolution of the right to employment without discrimination —collecting cases on Chinese, Filipinos, Negroes, Jews, Mexicans and women. The work which governmental administrative labor agencies have done is nothing less than monumental, and if I can do the paper I hope to do, it will show that we have made giant strides during the last ten years. Already, however, I'm beginning to believe strongly the FEPC bill should be amended to include "sex" along with its other "race, color, creed or national origin" factors. What do you think? Has anybody done anything along that line? It would be a shame to leave the women out of so broad a statute designed to plug up the holes of present protective legislation re employment.

In the meantime a course in Federal Income Tax is literally splitting my head. On the theory a gal must be good in a number of fields I let myself in for the hardest course in Law School, and if you don't think it takes everything I've got, you should see my study schedule which begins at 8:00 a.m. and with minor interruptions continues until 11:00 P.M.

The most thrilling of all, however, is a course in International Law and Relations with Dr. Hans Kelsen, Austrian authority on the League of Nations and now Dumbarton Oakes. This is a seminar in addition to Law School work, given over in the Political Science Department. So, just in case you want me for your secretary when you go into UNRRA[13] I'm trying to educate myself a little.

In the meantime, I-House has become a bee-hive of study and discussion in preparation for the San Francisco Conference. As Chairman (or rather one of two co-chairman) of our Wednesday evening discussion

13. When her Howard University job ended, Lina Ware had spoken of applying to, among other places, the United Nations Relief and Rehabilitation Administration, a wartime agency that was already at work overseas. Realizing the personal and professional reasons why she should not think of leaving the country, she also worried that by not serving where the action was she would miss the greatest experience of her generation. In the end, she went back to Howard.

table, we have outlined a most imposing program starting with Dumbarton Oaks, coming through the New Mexico Conference, Bretton Woods, and ending up with the background and significance of San Francisco conference.[14] This is our I-House theme for the month of April, and all House activities are pointed toward the conference. At last, a little respite from the problem of "being colored" has allowed me to turn my attention to the international picture with more than backhanded curiosity.

Not to neglect domestic issues, we've conjured up the cutest panel you ever saw—it's called the International House Panel, and is made up of a Jew, a Negro, a Spanish speaking American, a Chinese girl and a Nisei just back from Topas. We all live in the same cottage at I-House and are grand friends. Our panel's principle theme is "Breaking Down Barriers" from the point of view of the minority. We're all about the same size and utterly individual—which makes a very attractive showing. Our responses have been enthusiastic and we have been invited by groups in Oakland, Berkeley and San Francisco. Just our appearance has educational value, so we have timed everything, even to the clothes we wear, who will run discussion at what group. We call it "strategy and techniques" [she continues with more details, after which a page is missing.].

Two years pass during which Murray is in law school in California working on a master's degree and serving very briefly as assistant attorney general for the state. During those years Lina Ware continues her consumer protection work as well as her teaching.

In response to popular pressure, demobilization progressed rapidly, as did postwar inflation. Labor troubles erupted as well as problems in Europe, leading to a controversial loan to Great Britain and an aid program for Greece and Turkey.

For a while the correspondence languished. On June 8, 1946, Murray wrote an enthusiastic letter about the Morgan decision wherein the Supreme Court outlawed segregation in interstate transportation, saying

14. The preliminary planning for a draft charter for the United Nations took place at Dumbarton Oaks, a study center in Washington, D.C. Plans for the World Bank and the International Development Fund were laid at a conference in Bretton Woods, New Hampshire.

that uniformity among the states was essential.[15] *The same letter suggests that they keep in touch better and notes that Ware had been appointed to President Truman's Emergency Food Committee. Murray assumes that she will represent minority opinion as well as that of consumers:*

so my concern about consumer representation was taken care of. I privately thought my concern about minority representation is also taken care of. Love, Lil Lamb

Now, back in New York, Murray reports that she has a job with the American Jewish Commission on Law and Social Action with an annual salary of $3,640. The job deals with employment and restrictive covenants, and she adds, "I am bubbling with good spirits." She is taking vitamins, minerals, and hormonal injections, and the central message of her letter is: "My main objective right now is to become a top-notch lawyer."

Murray's health had been a problem for a long time. During the worst of the Depression when she was struggling to get through Hunter College, she was often malnourished and under considerable stress.

In 1937, at the initiative of a friend, she had been admitted to Bellvue Hospital in New York, and during her stay there she examined her worries about her sexual nature in writing, and said that she hoped to move more toward her masculine side. At an early age she had begun to experience conflict and stress centered on her belief that she was a man trapped in a woman's body. She continued for years to explore the developing medical literature about hormones, thinking that they might help her. She discussed the possibility of homosexuality with the doctors; she knew that she was attracted to very feminine, often white, women, and she knew as well that despite numerous male friends and admirers, and a brief marriage, she was not physically attracted to men. This conflict would continue for the rest of her life and, along with her fear of insanity because her father had died in a mental hospital, and the general fears of rejection and color prejudice that all black people harbored, constituted the "demons" of which she often spoke.

Here and elsewhere she describes her various physical ailments in detail.

15. *Morgan v. Com of Va.* 328 U.S. 373 (1946).

→} May 3, 1947

Beloved Skipper.

Your very sad letter[16] finds a very chastened and wiser Pixie. I rocked along last week, taking things in my stride, so I thought, until I ran into an adhesion which formed a partial obstruction. [She goes on to report her symptoms in gruesome detail.]

While I'm thrilled to be out of the hospital without a second incision, I'm having a time of it harnessing my drive to the incapacitated body. Have healed sufficiently to walk without pain, but it's so hard to remember not to lift books and the typewriter and trays and all the necessary movements one is accustomed to. I find I don't know the meaning of Patience after all. Oh well, the one lucky break of 1947 is the fact that I was covered by Blue Cross Hospitalization—both surgical and hospital service and that I was discharged the day the free coverage expired [. . .].

I'm by-passing North Carolina until I'm completely under my own steam again. I guess you read of the Reconciliation Tour which tested the Morgan decision in North Carolina, Virginia, and Tennessee, and which was brain trusted from this end by a number of us; also about the young Negro orderly from a Baltimore hospital who went to Dunn, N.C. to visit his mother for Easter, but was shot and killed by a RR conductor following an argument in which he refused or resisted orders to move to the Jim Crow train? And perhaps I told you of being invited to Durham to speak on April 24 under the auspices of a local Negro sorority who had hired the B.N. Duke auditorium but who were obliquely warned by Dr. J. E. Shepard against "controversial material" and whose President informally suggested that I speak on an innocuous subject like the "Negro Business Woman," so that I would avoid such controversial matters and thereby insure the sorority of getting the auditorium for future activities.[17] I promptly wired cancellation of the speech, and wiped the dust of Durham off my feet. I have informed my Mother I will come home if she

16. Ware's "very sad letter" has not surfaced.

17. The B. N. Duke Auditorium was on the campus of the North Carolina College for Negroes (now North Carolina Central University), the first state-supported liberal arts college for African Americans in the United States. Since it depended on the state legislature, the school's administration was very cautious.

wants me to help her settle her affairs, but that otherwise I won't be that way anytime soon.

I particularly appreciate the criticism of my letter to the U of C, blunt as you felt it was.[18] I can take things like that from you because there's an affinity there and I know yours is an objectivity not unlinked with personal concern for the individual involved. Unfortunately for the status of my case, the letter has already gone without the suggested changes which I would have accepted wholeheartedly had they gotten here. I can see with hindsight how the criticisms you make are valid to the extent that parts of the letter can antagonize a faculty or members thereof who might have been inclined to do otherwise. So I'll just have to take it, whatever they decide.

The reference to creative writing was in response to Mr. McGovney's letter—a very sweet one—who urged me toward that field. I have received a letter from Dean Dickinson already in response to it—a friendly one—saying the faculty would give careful consideration to all my letters, but suggesting that I had a number of misconceptions which he would attempt to straighten out once he could get his desk load which piled up while he was East down a bit. Actually my shock no doubt led me into so suspicious a frame of mind that I didn't pull my punches, although I tried to end the letter in a friendly tone. The fact of distance and the necessity for correspondence instead of discussion with my faculty advisors no doubt is responsible in part for my failure to understand fully the implications of the faculty's decision. If they do reject me again, then the only alternative from the East would seem to be to have all my higher education credits evaluated toward a PhD degree here at Columbia and mark U of C. down to experience—with a lesson in patience and prudence for me. The thing that makes me a fighter is the thing that hinders

18. "The criticism of my letter" refers to an intemperate letter Murray had written to the dean of the Boalt School of Law with respect to credits for work done there. She had sent a copy to Ware, who found it inappropriate for the matter at hand and tried to suggest to her the virtues of moderation and consideration for faculty sensitivity. Ware spelled out her reasons for thinking faculty members would be offended by the letter and concluded, "I just mean to say that I think your case would be stronger if you stick to the main point simply and use a minimum of argumentation and briefly."

me from being a diplomat and a statesman. So maybe I had better temper this fighting spirit.

I've read carefully Secretary Marshall's report to the American people, and I listened intently to every word of Henry Wallace's broadcast upon his return, and find myself in a very sad state of mind.[19] Wallace moved me deeply and I wish that he were sufficiently free of the "left wing" identification to help bring unity of liberal forces within PCA [Progressive Citizens of America] and ADA [Americans for Democratic Action] and then set up an independent third party movement for 1948. A large protest vote in 1948 would warn the two old parties they cannot kick labor around and pursue a dangerous foreign policy and expect to remain in power. But Wallace's gratuitous support from the "left" may cost him the support of many sincere liberals who have been burned enough. [She continues with a discussion of the attack on the American Jewish Congress and the general problem of being accused of Communist connections.] Pixie.

In the first of several attempts to make a living as a lawyer, Pauli begins with high hopes in 1948, an election year. Harry Truman had become president when FDR died in April 1945—and is now running for reelection. Henry Wallace, whom FDR had replaced as his vice presidential running mate in 1944, is forming the Progressive Party, and Governor Strom Thurmond of South Carolina is organizing the States' Rights ("Dixiecrat") Party.

⇥ 338 Chauncey St.
Brooklyn 33, New York
March 6, 1948
Dear Skipper:
It's a long way from Fulton Street to Broadway, but I should think that six months as a law clerk in a grass roots law office ought to be enough punishment for a lifetime. Thank goodness this particular aspect of it is

19. Secretary Marshall is General George C. Marshall, secretary of state under President Truman, and Murray's reference is to his plan for the reconstruction of Western Europe. Henry Wallace, former vice president (1941–45), was planning a third party.

over. I'm so tired of being a whipping boy for other people's doings and not being able to answer back—oh well, that's over, or will be on March 15.

On that date I join the staff of Richard L. Baltimore, 160 Broadway-BE-3 3844, N.Y.C. and as soon as I am admitted, [to the bar] which I hope is in May, I'll be managing attorney; an increase in pay, better working library, my own office, and a more challenging intellect with whom to work.

I think of you often and think it's about time for a gab session. There's so much I want to ask what you think of Wallace's Third Party business; whether you don't think Chester Bowles[20] makes a lot of sense with his administrator's approach to international problems; whether Truman's Civil Rights program and activities are part of an election year maneuver or whether they are sincere; whether you aren't very discouraged about the three Supreme Court justices (two of whom were on our side) disqualifying themselves in the restrictive covenant cases, whether the Sipuel case[21] won't be another dead duck; what's happening to the Howard Law School—is it going down or up? I hear conflicting stories, and on into the night.

Dark Testament is competing in a poetry contest. Wish it luck.

Also managed to send a few pieces to Arna Bontemps for try-out in the new anthology he and Langston Hughes are editing for Doubleday. Have you read Red Wine First, by Nedra Trye? Do you own it? Let me know.

What's with you? What's with the farm? How many puppies? I lost one with distemper. He had it when I got him and went through all the stages until finally convulsions—nothing helped, not even sulfa or penicillin.

20. Chester Bowles (1901–86) was a distinguished New Dealer who had made a fortune in business in his youth and thereafter established a record for liberal political action in a variety of posts. Ware had chaired the executive committee for consumer protection when Bowles headed the Office of Price Administration. See Howard B. Schaffer, *Chester Bowles: New Dealer in the Cold War* (Cambridge: Harvard University Press, 1993).

21. Ada Sipuel (1924–95), after much effort, won the right to be admitted to the University of Oklahoma Law School. She told her own story in *A Matter of Black and White: The Autobiography of Ada Lois Sipuel Fisher* (Norman: University of Oklahoma Press, 1996).

He fought so hard to live. I wonder where Toni is—I hope he got a good home. Did you get many lambs this season? Did the big snows and the cold make it hard for them to live? Did you get any help on the farm?

Saw myself in the movies the other day in a little short called "First." Got a nice surprise. It wasn't bad at all. Have also been playing around with a radio series called "The Visiting Psychiatrist" which consists of a psychiatrist and three interrogators over WEVD. Every once in a while I'm one of the interrogators. Radio is a lot of fun, I find, so I'm taking advantage of opportunities to develop it as a hobby.

Despite the protest at a law clerk's lot, I've had some very satisfying experiences recently. Several of my little memorandums and briefs have not gone entirely unrewarded and the judges have occasionally complimented my boss on them. The other day we won a particularly important victory. The Civil Service Commission revoked the certification of a young patrolman—James Europe, Jr. (you may remember the fame of his father, Jim Europe, as a band leader during the first world war) and questioned his civil service status on the lists for Fireman and Car Cleaner, on the ground that he had been engaged in "Communist activities" on the West Coast during 1941. The fact is he was fighting the jim crow policy of one of the seamen's unions who tried to pull him off the ship because of their unwritten taboo on Negroes as members of the union. I drew the papers for a mandamus proceeding in the Supreme Court to review the decision of the Civil Service Commission and to have a complete presentation of the evidence which the CSC had not done.

Their lawyer took one look at our papers, called us up and told us the Commission is reversing itself, reinstating our man with back pay. It has been a real experience of elation because it's the first fight on principle I've had my teeth into since turning back to law. That kind of thing makes the drudgery worth while.

[A long paragraph reports on the activities of a number of Pauli's friends who share her views, their names no longer identifiable.] Oh heck—this letter is such a poor substitute for a conversation. Can't you do something about it? On my law clerk's salary I can't yet. Best regards to Mrs. Coates[22] and to Gardiner. Love

22. Mrs. Coates was Lina and Gardiner's longtime housekeeper, whom they also regarded as a trusted friend.

On July 16, 1948 Lina suggests that Pauli write a "modern Paul Bunyan series"—stories of her adventures. She adds that she and Gardiner have, almost by accident, bought a 375-acre farm near Bull Run on which they plan to raise cattle. A disastrous fire when there was no insurance put an end to this project a few years later.

Through her connection with the Office of Price Administration and her former student, Mary Gresham, who worked for the OPA, Ware had been invited to Puerto Rico in 1944 to discuss community involvement in public policy. She had been enchanted by the Puerto Ricans she met, whom she perceived as being remarkably engaged in self-help, and began teaching there regularly in the summer. In time this experience would lead to her lifelong involvement with Latin America. Writing to Murray, she reports on her "usual tour of duty in Puerto Rico" and offers an analysis of the economic and political situation there. An eighteen-page letter is evidence of the truth of her niece's comment, "Lina liked to get at the root of things."

Two southern women, leaders in the Women's Society of the Methodist Church, came to Murray with a proposal that she should compile the state laws dealing with race and color so that the women in their church societies in each state could know their own situation before they began work to improve race relations. At the outset the goal was a pamphlet that could be circulated widely. Murray's astonishing capacity for hard work yielded a manuscript of more than 700 pages. In the days before photocopiers this involved a great deal of hand copying from statute books. The Methodist women were initially dismayed, but, impressed by what Murray had done, took a deep breath and continued to support her while they wondered how they could afford to publish the work. The chart Ware speaks of was part of that research. Murray also sends a draft of the book for comment and editorial suggestions.

Ware, meantime, is working hard to persuade members of the AAUW to support antisegregation efforts, and her letter shows something about where well-intentioned white middle-class women activists were on this issue at midcentury. The closing paragraph urging Pauli to visit is a refrain in many letters.

→ Vienna, Virginia

July 6, 1949

Dear Pauli,

Many thanks for the chart of segregation and civil rights laws. It is grand. Are additional copies available? If so, would you send one to Miss Marjorie Temple, American Association of University Women, 1634 Eye Street, Washington, D.C.

You see why she wants it. She has to help advise the southern branches how to cope with the AAUW policy and their local laws.

I may say that the AAUW convention did better than I had dared to hope. I felt sure that the vote would be okay—but I thought the opposition would muster more than 68 votes as there was a strong "local autonomy" sentiment quite independent of the issue. Apparently the only real negative effort at the convention came from ye olde Washington branch & the Texas delegation, with a few others playing along. Some of the other southern gals were cooperative but genuinely puzzled as to how they could actually implement the policy. The gal from Alabama, in the face of current Klan activity, didn't at all see how she could make headway and hold her organization. Just before she came to convention, night riders had invaded a girl scout leadership training camp for Negro leaders, taken out the two white women who were in charge (they got out of the state fast) and bust[ed] up the camp. The current drive seems to be directed as much—perhaps even more—against any whites that show signs of cooperation as against Negroes who are "uppity." Most of the AAUW gals are not martyrs by temperament—in fact they probably regard martyrdom as a rather poor technique. So the situation isn't simple. On the other hand, the Virginia delegation was solidly on the right side, the key speech was made by the regional vice president for the southeastern region, and the opposition speech by the president of the Washington branch offended practically everybody. I suspect that with the U. of Ky. breaking down and with things happening pretty fast in Missouri that the good current tactic may be to work hard on the border area and drive an effective wedge between it and the deep south.

Incidentally, it seems to me that the Interior Dept and the St. Louis recreation director have been very stupid to force the issue first on swimming pools. Anybody knows that pools are one of the hardest things to crack. I don't know what the present situation is, but not so long ago a high school pool in one of the New Jersey Oranges was closed because they couldn't keep Negroes out and they wouldn't have them in. If you get that kind of feeling in the Oranges what do you expect in D.C.? It certainly seems to me that they would have done better to press harder on the other less difficult facilities and start by using the pools on alternate days or something like that. Now they have made a hasty retreat, confirmed the belief that the community mores are inviolable and probably good, and lost the momentum that was gathering. If they were really prepared to carry through, they should have provided an adequate police guard and have let it be known, if trouble was started that the pools would be closed to all until they could be operated without disorder.

However, as an historian, I always remind myself that violence is nearly always counter-revolutionary: the effort of the former haves to regain what the changes of the times have taken from them.

How are you making out in your new establishment? I trust that business is reasonably good and that the wolf keeps from the door and family complications are within bounds, and the law feels good, and you get what time for writing you desire.

Incidentally I was pleased to find your name included in the new anthology of verse by Negroes, and liked the selection [. . .].

The report that we were traveling the Alaska Highway this summer turned out to have been exaggerated. We did plan to—in fact we were due to drive a new station wagon up for the son of the Governor of Alaska. But he wrote that the cars that come over the highway arrived in such a state—the condition of the highway being terrible—that he wasn't going to have his new car wrecked so please ship by boat. That finished our trip, because obviously we couldn't carry out our original idea of buying a car and selling it up there if it were going to be all broken up when we got there. And then we figured that if the cars were wrecks on arrival the passengers would be somewhat the worse for wear too. So we dropped the Alaska venture, are puttering around here until the first of August, taking a canoe trip near here, perhaps Maine again in August, and calling this the lazy summer. It's hot enough to make me wish that I had joined the Grenfell mission to Labrador! Now I know why I have been running away to the tropics every summer.

Any chance of your paying us a visit—longer than the last time, preferably.

Yours, Skipper

While Pauli is having a hard time making a living and sustaining her enthusiasm for the law, she has impressed people in the New York Liberal Party, who put her up for the City Council seat from Brooklyn's Tenth Senatorial District, in which she lived. She was encouraged by the fact that Maida Springer[23] had run for the New York assembly, and, though she lost, had succeeded in giving visibility to minority women in politics. Murray throws herself enthusiastically into the effort and sends her friends—including the Ware-Meanses—a series of bulletins titled "Pixies in Politics," reporting on her campaign. A good many friends contribute money to her campaign.

→ September 5, 1949

[Lina congratulates Pauli on the decision to run for public office and sends a check.] I am delighted that you decided to run. It doesn't surprise me that the pixies are in there pitching. If you don't wear yourself down too much you ought to get a lot out of the campaign in the way of fun, prestige, and business. I wish I could be a fly on the wall and watch the process.

This is one of several times in their relationship when Ware, sensing a need to bolster Murray's morale, writes often, providing support and enthusiasm.

→ Vienna, Virginia

October 15, 1949

Dear Pixie: It is delightful and wonderful to see the political front unfolding. Go easy, though. What if you should be elected! I cherish and chortle over each bulletin. This is the first time I have felt like getting into

23. Maida Springer was a close friend of Murray's; for more on her, see the comments preceding Murray's letter of April 22, 1950, in Chapter 2.

a political fight myself since I cut my political baby teeth campaigning for Al Smith way back in 1928. [. . .] More power to you. Skipper.

Throughout the campaign, Lina continues to provide encouragement.

✈ New Virginia
October 29 [1949]
Dear Pixie:

We love it, we love it, we love it! And we love you dearly—and are grateful for the ringside reports. The high point to date is the position piece by Harvard—Comment: it has *everything*. Gardiner and I held our sides and practically rolled on the floor with mirth and delight over that one.

All that I wish is that I had a television set and you were being televized. Or better still that Brooklyn was handy enough for me to join the "crusade."

You said last summer that the big time politicos hadn't caught up with the young district hence you as a candidate. At the present rate, you're soon going to be having to duck the flying knives.

We are counting on a personal appearance in New Virginia when The Day is passed. [. . .] More power to you. Skipper

✈ Vienna, Virginia
Nov. 6, 1949
Dear Pixie,

I've just been discussing matters with the grand master of the elves, leprechauns, and other little people. He assures me that they have arranged to station a little person in every voting booth to whisper in the ear of each uncertain voter, "Row D," and to pinch any voter who starts to stray anywhere else. So if Pixie fails to get a majority of the votes, she should take up the matter with the fairy leadership so that they will improve their organization before the next time around.

From the bulletins and clippings, I gather that the worst you are likely to do would be spectacular. Good going. And whatever happens, you should have a booming law practice from now on. If you survive the sleepless nights as you seem to be doing—it will have been a very fine thing to have done that campaign.

Then too—the cat you introduced into the New Virginia household wanted to do her bit for you, so she caught a rabbit and brought it to the house, foot and all. I told her that the postman might not like to carry such a fresh rabbits foot, but that you would appreciate the spirit.

Prayer rugs arranged, fingers crossed—and all preparations made to be surprised at nothing—for after all this is Pixie's campaign and where Pixie is concerned anything can happen.

Affectionately, Skipper

Encouragement continues to flow right up to election eve. Murray does not win, but she does better than anyone except possibly herself expected. Meanwhile Ware is working and observing the political scene in Virginia, especially with respect to racial issues.

→ Vienna, Virginia
Nov. 10 [1949]
Dear Pixie

Congratulations on a fine showing. By the look of the figures, still incomplete, in the edition of the N.Y. Times that reached here, you are outstanding among the Liberal candidates—and the Liberal party rather than the Republican Party is rapidly becoming the loyal opposition in New York City.

It was too much to expect that with Lehman[24] heading the Democratic ticket and the issue made Fair Deal or rejection of the welfare state, many of the potentially Liberal Democrats would split their tickets. It's too bad, though, that the Tammany entrenchment has been deepened. The composition of the City Council is sadly top heavy. For all its obvious faults, P.R. [proportional representation] gave at least some variety to the membership. By the look of the election, New Yorkers will have to do as Virginians: concentrate on trying to capture the primaries.

We aren't doing too badly. We—i.e. Miller [Francis Pickens Miller]—failed by a substantial margin to get the nomination for governorship but

24. Herbert H. Lehman (1878–1963) served in a variety of important posts in government, including as governor of New York, and as director general of UNRRA. In 1949 he was elected as a Democrat to the United States Senate, where he served until 1957.

pulled up a strong vote. He will now probably run for Howard Smith's seat in Congress and will stand a good chance to get it as the district has a lot of northern Va., Washington suburbs voters. That will put him in line to contest [Harry F.] Byrd, or his nominee, for Byrd's senate seat in 1952. Meantime, the new Virginia democrats will probably capture the Fairfax County democratic organization next Thursday at the caucus.

The greatest show of strength ironically enough, was the Va. vote not to repeal the poll tax. The machine tried to pull a fast one by presenting some very complicated voting amendments that look on the face like the poll tax repeal we were waiting for but actually gave the legislature power to [invent] any other restrictions that it could dream up. So the League of Women Voters and other good citizens around the state put on an educational campaign and the amendments were killed by a better than 3-1 vote. In other words, the Va. machine that depends on being able to operate behind its own iron curtain is being pulled out into the open and when the voters can see it they slap it down.

There is a lot of handwriting on Virginia walls!

When do we see you? I'll be back from Greensboro Sunday night. The latch string is then out for any and much time. If Thanksgiving looks good, we may be able to provide entertainment with some of the delegates of the FAO [Food and Agriculture Organization] conference.

Honor to all Pixies

Skipper

2

THE COLD WAR,

McCARTHYISM, AND

CIVIL RIGHTS

The end of her venture as a candidate for office and the completion of the great compilation of state laws affecting discrimination, to which she returned after her electoral defeat, left Murray somewhat downhearted, although she remained much involved in party politics. At midcentury she was still having trouble making a decent living.

American history is littered with times when one or another group of people has been seen by others as endangering the country. The Alien and Sedition Acts of 1798, limiting freedom of speech and of the press and attacking aliens, were an early example. In the early nineteenth century a political party was organized in response to the growing popularity and supposed influence of the Masonic order. Then there was the American Party, usually called the Know-Nothing Party, created in opposition to Catholicism or to Irish immigrants, or both. Not much later, southern states expelled abolitionists, and, once the Civil War began, in both the North and the South opposition to the war was considered to be treason. In the late nineteenth century freedpeople suffered attacks and the Chinese were denied entry to the country (or, if admitted, used virtually as slave labor). The United States government made war on the Mormons, presumably because they practiced polygamy. The so-called Red Scare in 1919, which led to the deportation of some radicals and the jailing of others, came at a time of social turmoil, as members of labor unions and black soldiers home from the war were involved in riots and protests of many kinds. The stage was set for a revival of the Ku Klux Klan in the 1920s.

Beginning in the 1930s, the search for Communists, and by extension all progressives, began to heat up with the creation of the House Committee on Un-American Activities, chaired by Martin Dies. Politicians used accusations of disloyalty for their own purposes. One result was the trial of Alger Hiss, brought about by the vigorous efforts of Richard Nixon, who had been elected to Congress from California in 1946 when he defeated Jerry Voorhis, one of the most thoughtful progressives in Congress, by charging that he had Communist connections. Perhaps the anti-Communist crusade could muster so much support in the wake of World War II because of the number of what seemed like threats in a time of trouble in international relations. On one side of the world, the United States was concerned about the intentions of the Soviet Union; on the other, the Communist North Koreans, instigated by China and the Soviet Union, invaded South Korea, provoking a military response from the United States and the United Nations. Whatever the complex causes, this outbreak of intolerance affected both Murray and Ware, though in different ways and to different degrees.

↠ January 26, 1950

Dear Skipper:

I have been thinking about you, now that the compilation is over and done. [. . .]

The Hiss verdict has left me a little sad, although I knew nothing of Hiss until I began to follow his trial.[1] Because the Post editorial seems to catch the spirit of the thing, I am sending it along.

I am having organizational growing pains. The Citizens Union of which I'm a member now has joined with the League of Women Voters to carry on a campaign for permanent personal registration in New York State. A bill has been introduced into the Albany legislature providing for same. The Liberal Party, of which I am also a member is unalterably opposed to it in principle. I'm torn with conflict, because it appears on surface to be a good thing, although I admit that the administration of

1. Alger Hiss, (1904–96), a senior State Department official, was accused by Whittaker Chambers, a magazine editor and confessed Communist Party courier, of being a Communist and of having given information to the Soviet Union. Richard Nixon, then a member of Congress trying to build a national reputation, took up the cry against Hiss. A trial ended with a hung jury, but, indicted again on grounds of perjury, Hiss was the subject of a second trial that preoccupied the media for many months. The guilty verdict in the second trial saddened and confused many liberals. The argument as to whether he was guilty or not continues to the present day.

such a procedure in the hands of the two major parties may be used to stifle the enrollment (and therefore the growth) of a minority party.

Am active in the Lib. Party State legislative committee and have taken a hand in drafting bills to be introduced in the legislature, i.e. proposed amendments to the housing redevelopment laws to prevent segregation, exclusion and discrimination on basis of race, etc., and bill outlawing restrictive covenants. Am learning something about the politics of introducing bills etc.

Glad to see that Frances Williams bobbed up again as legislative assistant to Senator Lehman.[2] Pained to see a reported statement by Frank P. Graham that he would vote against an FEPC bill with enforcement powers and that he was for voluntary cooperation.

You said two years ago the principle for FEPC had been won. Do you feel the same way now? Tell me also, is there anything so terrible in the Equal Rights Amendment if it has a protective provision saving present and future special protective legislation.[3] I'm a little confused over the issue, although Lehman voted against it together with a gang of Southern Democrats.

I also think the Powell-Roosevelt exchange was unnecessary and that Powell did the "Race" no service by saying that he could go no further; he was as far as he could go as a Negro in our generation. Look at Harvard and the United States Supreme Court is only one step away. We intend to go as far as our abilities will take us.[4]

I have just finished looking over my financial picture for 1949. If

2. Frances Williams, an African American, was a social worker with the YWCA. Lina had brought her into government as a staff person at the National Defense Council, and together they had made the clerical staff more diverse. She became a friend. When Herbert Lehman was elected to the Senate, she found a job on his staff.

3. The old-line feminist movement had long opposed the proposed Equal Rights Amendment, fearing that it might wipe out hard-won protective legislation covering women and children, and several of the women's organizations still held to that view. Years later, Murray would confront the issue when she was a founding member of the National Organization for Women.

4. Adam Clayton Powell Jr. (1908–72), an African American minister, was a member of Congress from New York. Apparently he had had some exchange with Eleanor Roosevelt. There is no report of such a controversy in the *New York Times*.

income is an index of ability I had better start collecting garbage. They guys make more than I do. Oh well—

Warmest regards to Gardiner.

Write soon to a sometimes discouraged [Pixie]

By now the friendship has endured for eight years, and Lina has become accustomed to the ups and downs of Pauli's moods. The news that the state laws compilation will really be published changes Murray's tone remarkably.

⚘ March 31, 1950

Dear Skipper:

Hail the coming of Spring. If I had answered your note Friday, I should have no doubt announced that I was taking down my shingle and applying for the first baby-sitting job I could find. Luckily, I didn't so now the news is encouraging.

What I couldn't tell you during the waiting stage was that there was a very real danger the Women's Division manuscript would remain in moth balls and never see the light of publication because of the prohibitive cost. They had thought of all kinds of substitutes, such as publishing a brief summary or a pamphlet little longer than my introductory "Scope Note." However, they have just completed their over-all committee meetings and the word is that the Women's Division will subsidize the publication up to 2,000 copies and that it will sell at about $4.00 per copy. They hope to have it off the press around mid-summer.[5] Glory be!

Now I need to compile a list of organizations which will be willing to promote the sale of copies within their ranks. If you have a few in mind, save them for me until when I see you.

Aside from my three Aunts being ill at the same time and my clients losing their jobs and having no money things have been going along wonderfully! [...]

Twenty-two days later Murray's letter exhibits a familiar pattern: when she has a big decision to make, she lays out the issues and asks for

5. The manuscript was published, under the title *States' Laws on Race and Color*, by the Women's Division of Christian Service in Cincinnati, Ohio, in 1950.

Ware's advice and guidance. These queries usually lead to a judicious, carefully worded reply. This long letter illustrates the systematic way Pauli Murray analyzed problems, especially those related to her career development.

Maida Springer, who appears often in these pages, is Pauli Murray's close friend, whom she first met when they worked together on the Odell Waller case. Springer's household, which included her very lively mother, is one of Murray's favorite places of refuge. In 1945 Springer, who was in Washington for a meeting and was incensed by the amount of discrimination she encountered everywhere she went, was invited to The Farm. She went reluctantly. In an interview many years later, she recalled that meeting:

> In spite of Dr. Ware's fine reputation, I approached the visit [. . .] with acute wariness [. . .]. I expected that my visit would be one more expression of thinly veiled condescension on the part of my host [. . .]. I had never been more in error in my entire life. Dr. Ware [. . .] had clear, direct eyes and said "I'm delighted that you are here. Welcome to the farm" [. . .]. The rapid fire conversation that afternoon seemed to span the universe, for the first time that week my guard was down and I found myself treated as one of a group of interesting personalities sharing equally in the hospitable climate of the "The Farm."

> Since that fortuitous day, thirty-six years ago, Dr. Ware [. . .] became my majority of one [. . .].[6]

So it was that Maida Springer joined Pauli Murray in viewing Lina Ware as a guide and mentor. From that point forward, she too was a recipient of Ware's concern and generosity.

Two of Murray's aunts have left North Carolina and are living with her. Each has a tiny pension, but they are both dependent on her in many ways.

✦ April 22, 1950
Dear Skipper:
Tried to reach you by telephone today, but you were out. Perhaps it is just as well, because it compels me to think this thing out by writing it—

6. Ruth Edmonds Hill, ed., *The Black Women Oral History Project*, vol. 7 (Westport, Conn.: Meckler, 1991), 147ff.

which may be sounder in the long run. Would you act as a sponge for the moment?

First of all, let me say that that prayer rug you must have been using on my behalf has been atomic. Business started picking up the very next week and has been booming (for me) ever since. The temporary outlook is encouraging.

The revised charts (Women's Division) are out in a color job and look very snassy. Also they have gotten out a little folder advertising the book (for internal consumption) which looks very neat on the outside but which is very flat on the inside—lacks umph and does the mss an injustice. However, for outside promotion, new copy might be inserted that would tease the appetite for the book.

Most important, the first batch of proof arrived last week, so the gals mean business.

This is not the purpose of this letter, however. Yesterday a friend of mine who is an active attorney of the American Civil Liberties Union, Walter Frank, called me and told me there was an opening in the Union for an Associate Staff Counsel, a new job being created, to divide some of the legal work which is now being handled. The present salary set by the budget is $4200.00, but it would not be difficult to have them up it a bit if they get the right person. The staff person and some members of the Board apparently are aware of some of my work and seemed pleased when my name was mentioned for the job. I was invited to submit my qualifications.

If I do submit qualifications, there is a very real chance I would get the job. They are actually looking for someone who would make a career of it, rather than an ambitious young man who wants to use the position to make contacts and as a spring board for something else. George Rundquist in talking with me about it via telephone yesterday, indicated that he knew the general field of Civil Liberties had been my special concern for some time, and that frankly they needed someone in the organization who had some imagination. He stated that the Scopes case has become an ACLU matter because Roger Baldwin had happened to clip a news story of the trial, and had urged the organization to become interested in the case.

Naturally, this indirect offer, has caused me some excitement. Maida and I have talked it over and her thinking seems to be as follows: It has many advantages and few disadvantages. (1) Financial security and breathing space which I have needed for some time and which is especially important at the present when I have two elderly partial dependents to think of with all the attendant problems and emergencies which can arise at advanced age. (2) prestige value which is almost an ideal next step for me, in that my connection with the ACLU will attach a dignity to my professional work which I cannot get as fast going it alone as a single practitioner, and which will be good for my record, (3) contact with legal minds of stature and integrity which I have missed during these years of legal isolation in practicing alone and with general practice, (4) a good springboard for the next step after two or three years with ACLU if I want to get out of it at that time. In other words, assuming I wanted to return to private practice in two or three years, my chances of getting connected with the kind of firm that meets my concept of success would be better than anything I could get by trying to make a change from a single practice, (5) an opportunity to play the whole field of Civil Liberties which would not be possible in an organization like NAACP or American Jewish Congress, together with an opportunity for study and brief writing which appears to be one of my better trained abilities—allowing opportunity for appellate work, which I cannot get in much detail through general practice, (6) general professional and organizational contact which I have lacked over the past three years.

The disadvantages seem to be these: (1) Am I ready for this step at this time? I have not had too intensive an experience in general practice, such as trial work, jury trials, etc. I had wanted to give myself two years in my own office to see whether I had what it takes. Suppose I became restive in a staff job; since the position demands that I give up my private practice, I would be unable to again start on the shoestring which catapulted me into private practice a year ago. On the other hand, if I let this opportunity go at a time when I am psychologically looking upward and feel that I *am* making a temporary go at private practice, would I ever get another opportunity "made-to-order" so to speak? Certainly my Cash Book entries are no recommendation to stay in private practice at the marginal level of the past 15 months. Nor is there a guarantee that this temporary upswing will continue long enough to take some of the financial pressure off of me. I might add here that it would be necessary for me to take in about $700.00 each and every month in order to run the office efficiently with clerical help and still clear $350.00 per month (which approximates the ACLU salary).

(2) This modest little practice is something which I have built from nothing, and nursed along like a baby. It is just beginning to show something of my initial investment in time and patience and painstaking study. I have been able to keep myself afloat against great odds. That, in itself, has given kind of inner confidence. If I leave it at this point before it pays off in a modest living, will I be a failure at private practice? That question is not an easy one to answer to myself. Once the die is cast there will be no coming back immediately. And stability is always a very real (or imagined) problem with me.

[She repeats some of her points and then goes on.] Another factor, of course, is that the ACLU has no doubt never employed a Negro woman on staff counsel, and this would have its own interesting facets.

I have tried to state the case as we mulled it over yesterday. Maida wanted particularly for you to know her thinking on the matter, because she feels that this would be an ideal step for me, but she wants to be sure that she is not overrating what she believes the ACLU status to be. [She ends by saying she has decided to submit her qualifications, but if Lina has reactions or thinks of things that have not occurred to them she would like to know.]

Lina takes the request for advice seriously and answers almost immediately with her own analysis of the pros, winding up with her advice.

→ The Ambassador
Atlantic City
April 26 [1950]
Dear Pixie
The letterhead indicates that I am dutifully attending the National Conference of Social Work in Atlantic City.

I can't add anything to the thoughts which you have had about the ACLU job. As usual you have done a good job of analysis in thinking it through. Of the points that seem to me relatively important the chance for professional association seems one deserving some priority. I have been aware of the professional loneliness and you might almost say, bare to bareness of your present situation. How much of a staff does ACLU have? How does it operate? What consultants does it use and how?

On the other side, the question of the actual kinds of experience that you would have raise questions in my mind. What is ACLU practice about assigning and handling cases? Does a lawyer carry a case through or do staff persons do "staff" work—i.e. preparation, looking up stuff etc while someone else actually "handles" the case? I think that your feel for getting a range of experience is good. But ACLU may be as good or better than your private practice for getting it.

On the whole, I think that the balance adds up on the ACLU side, probably. If you had not had the experience with ordinary, grubby, little people's problems I would say "no"—for your preoccupation with civil rights and liberties could have been limiting. But the time that you have put in since leaving the Am. Jewish Congress has given you a real experience in the practice of law at the grass roots. You know at first hand that most of most people's problems are bread and butter, and personal relations as well as marital etc. with this background, you now return to the civil rights & liberties field as your field for specialization without undue narrowing, it seems to me.

You say that the staff position would require your abandoning private practice altogether. I am surprised at that. I should think it would still permit your taking occasional cases on your own, provided that they did not cut in on the time which you owe the Association. Perhaps the actual mechanisms interfere—i.e. necessity of appearing in court on the court's time not yours. But apart from this I should not think that ACLU would forbid its lawyers to carry private cases out of hours—especially if they were not civil liberties cases.

On the question of prestige etc. of ACLU I have no clear knowledge at present. Certainly, the whole loyalty issue has made the question of civil liberties central. I haven't been following the actual role of ACLU currently.

While I sympathize with your desire to show yourself that you can swing a private practice & your reluctance to pull out just when some of your earlier investment of effort is paying off, I think that you have demonstrated your capacity to survive in that legal bull pen and that there is no need for you to undergo the strain of continuing to fight that battle. I was impressed the last time I saw you with how well your health & spirits were holding up, but at the same time with the strain that family situation was imposing on them. If you take a salaried job now it will certainly give you a kind of breathing and growing spell, free from the growing harassment of operating a complicated life too close to the margin.

Either way things break, it seems to me you will be okay. As you say, this is one of the first times when you have really had a *choice*. I don't think you will regret having sent in your qualifications to ACLU. If the job should not materialize, there is no essential loss, for the private practice experience still has much to offer—and doubtless something else will come along—

More power to you—as always—Best to Maida

Yours, Skipper

P.S. Tragic about Charlie Houston[7] but this is a warning to all devoted battlers not to wear themselves out while their potential continued usefulness is still great.

No one would discover from reading these letters that North Korea had invaded South Korea or that President Truman had committed U.S. troops to counter the invasion. Pauli Murray was, as she said, preoccupied with the gradual change in the Supreme Court's attitude toward Plessy v. Ferguson. *She follows the process with fascination and regularly shares her reactions with Lina.*

June 13, 1950

Dear Skipper:

I'm busy as all get out this morning, but must take time out to tell you I've just read the texts of the three segregation decisions.[8] I'm so excited I

7. Houston was a well-known workaholic, for whom fourteen- and sixteen-hour days were common. He felt there was so much to do, so little time to do it all. In early 1950 he had a heart attack, from which he seemed to be recovering. However, in May of that year he died, leaving his adored five-year-old son a message to the effect that the child should not think he had been deserted since his father had gone down fighting in order that his son would have a better life than he had, without prejudice or bias standing in his way.

8. On June 5, 1950, the Supreme Court issued three segregation-related decisions. Two involved graduate education, and one dealt with transportation. The Court

can't contain myself. The newspaper quotes didn't do justice to the implications of the language. If you haven't already read them, get hold of them by all means. In the world of mysticism, I would say the spirits of Harlan, Murphy and Rutledge must have been in such great evidence around the Court, they caught the spirit of the Harlan dissent, even if they gave lip service to "narrow decisions." They do not say they will not consider *Plessy v. Ferguson* at some future time,

> We cannot therefore, agree with respondents (State of Texas) that the doctrine of *Plessy v. Ferguson* . . . requires reaffirmance of the judgment below. Nor need we reach petitioner's contention that *Plessy v. Ferguson* should be reexamined in the light of contemporary knowledge respecting the purposes of the Fourteenth Amendment and the effects of racial segregation.

In other words, "we don't go as far as reexamining *Plessy* at this time—we can reach the desired result without drawing *Plessy* into the discussion."

The thrilling thing about these decisions is that for the first time, the Court has faced the psychological implications of segregation—the intangibles—squarely and has not retreated to legal technicalities to reaffirm a simple human right. The discussion on the U. of Texas Law School is magnificent. I react to it so strongly because some of the same arguments were used by one Pixie to stress the reason why it was important for a woman to attend Harvard School of Law. Furthermore, taking the three decisions together you will find your own theory about discrimination against the white person through discrimination—the theory

---

defined the general question as "To what extent does the Equal Protection Clause of the fourteenth amendment limit the power of a state to distinguish between students of different races in professional and graduate education in a state university?" In *Sweatt v. Painter* 329 U.S. 639 (1950) the Court held that the Equal Protection Clause of the Fourteenth Amendment required that the petitioner be admitted to the University of Texas Law School. In *McLauren v. Oklahoma State Regents for Higher Education et al.* 339 U.S. 637, 70 S.Ct. 851 (1950) the Court held that Oklahoma could not impose on a black student requirements different from those it imposed on all others. The decision in *Henderson v. United States et al.* 339 U.S. 816, 70 S.Ct. 813 (1950) held that the Interstate Commerce Commission had violated the law when it did not insist that a railroad not segregate its passengers in the dining area.

we discussed with reference to separating two friends—a white and a Negro—on a Southern train. All in all, it is a good job and now I feel confident that the Court can't retreat, but must go forward from case to case, until *Plessy* goes down the drain along with the *Dred Scott* decision. I think now it is a matter of timing of strategy to let the cases reach the court when public opinion is ripe. For this is surely as much a political decision as it is a legal one. It could have been made on legal grounds just as well 50 years ago.

Enough of my raving—the ACLU deal fell through. My price tag was too high. They decided to take somebody with less experience who would be eager to learn what they offered. It was disappointing at first because they seemed particularly eager to have me (Negro-woman) but in the long run I think I would have felt I gave up too much for immediate security. In another year with two or three years of practice under my belt, the [compilation of state laws] book off the press, and perhaps a law review article published, my own evaluation of myself will be better and should I want to take a salaried position I will be in a better bargaining position—if I survive, and I guess I will. [. . .]

What are your plans? How long will you be at the Farm before going to Boston, if your plan still remains to go there?

Write when you get around to it—and warm regards to Gardiner. Hurriedly,

While Murray was excited about the progress of the courts in matters of civil rights, her own experience and Ware's were with a different aspect of the problem. When the Second World War ended, the House Committee on Un-American Activities increased its vigilance, the Hiss case filled the newspapers, and Senator Joseph McCarthy went on a rampage against so-called Communists in government. In retrospect it is easy to see just how wild most of McCarthy's accusations were, but at the time few individuals or institutions stood up to him. The Cold War and the existence of the atomic bomb, along with a good deal of political bombast, had combined to create an atmosphere of fear that McCarthy played upon effectively. Anybody who had belonged to an organization even mildly critical of the status quo might be attacked. The following letter reveals a pattern that will repeat itself several times in Murray's life: a job for which she is well suited, and which she very much wants, eludes her for reasons about which she can only speculate. In discussing the situation, she reveals her systematic and persistent method of pursuing opportunities. It is a little puzzling, considering that the job is in the UN's Human Rights Division, that she does not appear to have appealed to Eleanor Roosevelt, whose standing in that area was perhaps greater than that of any other person.

Here and elsewhere Murray assumed that Ware would welcome every detail about her various job searches and their outcomes.

→ January 26, 1951

Dear Skipper:

[. . .] First, as to the UN position. It apparently has struck a bottleneck and is hanging fire for the moment. The nearest I can make out is that when my application reached the desk of the Assistant Secretary General together with a strong memorandum from the head of the Division of Human Rights recommending appointment, the question was raised why take on somebody for 6 months, losing same just when she is becoming valuable to the organization, when you can select someone from an underdeveloped country who can remain on in the organization? Suggest you think about that, etc. etc. And so the application had not been approved or rejected as of last knowledge.

At this point, several of my International House former house mates who are on the staff—the word is that UN is just one big International House some 20 years later—went into action with a little undercover work. It involved a friend who knew a friend who knew someone who worked in the budgetary end, who in turn was a good friend of the assistant to the assistant of the Asst. Secy-General in point. I am told by my friends after much unofficial after-hours telephoning and talking and showing of materials on me, etc. etc, that the promise was made that my citizenship would not be considered as a factor in my application. [She says she is third in line for the job. . . .]

So, all this has been maddening to me because for about ten days the prospects of immediate appointment were so imminent that I did not know whether to take on new cases, accept retainers, knock myself out with the office, or what. The latest advice from *unofficial sources* in and around the Personnel Office seem to be that as long as I do not have an outright letter of rejection, my chances are still extremely good. [. . .]

That's a rough sketch of the past three weeks. In the meantime, the latter half of 1950 was almost zero in the credit column, so financially I was in over my head and thoroughly disgusted with me and the law practice. Coupled with that a judge ruled against me on a case which no one could see how it was possible for me to lose, considering the overwhelming amount of documentary and oral evidence on my side of the case. [. . .] I had a sudden revulsion for the practice of law [. . .] lawyers usually say that unless you know the judge or have connections, you don't have much chance. But how can nearly 20,000 lawyers in New York know the judge? And furthermore if I have to know the judge to win my case I'll never win it. [. . .]

All in all, I have been taking a very dim view of this area of my profession of late. [She describes an opportunity to go to Puerto Rico which she had hesitated to take for several reasons.] All of us are in such a state of uncertainty, caution and fear that we are hesitant in handling unpopular cases, supporting unpopular causes [. . .]. Those of us who have been uncompromising in our fight against discrimination are particularly vulnerable because we are not sure that the loyalty experts are careful to distinguish between the "loyal opposition" and outright subversives.

This mood is the outgrowth of reading the reports of the Remington trial[9], the aftermath of the Hanley letter, and personal accounts of two people I know who were in line for important appointments but failed to survive the check. I wonder how many home front casualties there are of the cold and lukewarm wars [. . .].

Six days later her mood is not much improved.

→ Thursday, February 1, 1951

Dear Skipper:

[She recapitulates much of what was in the previous letter, and goes on to say that her practice is picking up. But she details all the struggles of

9. In 1948 William Remington had been accused of giving information about the Manhattan Project (the atomic weapons project) to Elizabeth Bentley, a confessed Communist spy. At the time Murray wrote this letter, he had just been indicted on perjury charges.

independent practice and the frustration of finding that the indexer for her big book of state laws was holding up publication. When she investigates, she discovers that a series of disasters had struck the indexer, who says dolefully that perhaps the whole project had been cursed. Her frustration about the book possibly darkened her view of the world scene. She goes on:]

Furthermore when one looks around one does not see a generation of rebels and revolutionaries to supplant the generation of our youth. It is as if such a generation were non-existent and we who have grown older [she is forty-one] have become paralyzed [. . .]. I conclude that a man like Byrnes[10] who is not the very worst example, would prefer to be conquered by a foreign enemy than to give up their racial superiority.

The sign of the times is illustrated by a big black and white sign on the street signpost at the corner of Maiden Lane and Broadway which directs one to Public Shelter and points in the direction of Wall Street. Last Saturday we had an air raid siren test which almost nobody heard. Every time my folks [her aunts] see a flash in the sky (brought on by contact with icy rails of the elevated trains) they wonder if the Atomic Bomb has arrived and demand of me why I don't get out of the Wall Street area before it is too late. They, of course, are segments of the confused and perplexed public which gets a garbled idea of the news by radio and give me a daily interpretation which makes me wonder if we both read the same papers.

Skipper, I'm sorry this letter has to be so doleful, and I know in my heart that the mood will change—but this is the result of a dreamer trying to confront realities, and at such times pouring it out on paper is the only thing that eases the pressure [. . .].

In the summer of 1951 Ware's father, in Massachusetts, is ill. She spends a great deal of time with him, taking her work along so that she need not feel pushed to hurry home. Murray expresses concern but is almost immediately back to her own worries.

10. James Byrnes of South Carolina (1879–1972), who had been a member of both the House and the Senate and, briefly, a justice of the Supreme Court, was secretary of state, appointed by Harry Truman, from 1945 to 1947. In 1951 he was elected governor of South Carolina.

→| June 15, 1951

Dear Skipper:

[The letter opens with details about a plan for Murray and Maida Springer to spend part of the summer in New Jersey, away from the pressures of life in New York. Murray then goes on to discuss her plan for expanding Springer's opportunities. As she sees the situation, Springer, who does not have a college degree, consistently underrates herself in relation to her friend even though she is an extremely talented labor organizer and an all-around capable person. Murray's plan calls for Springer to spend a year at Ruskin College in England on a union scholarship. When it turns out that the scholarship is given only to people under thirty-five, Murray tries to find an alternative scholarship. Springer did go, with aid from the American Scandinavian Foundation.]

As for myself, Maida and I had tea with Mrs. R. on Wednesday past. Naturally, she asked me what how things were. I told of the ILO [International Labor Organization] pending [job] application and the difficulty in French as one of the requirements. She feels that it should not be too great a handicap because the way we teach French in the United States is not conducive to actually speaking and understanding the language [. . .]. Most important she said "Do you think it would help any if I wrote to the head of the ILO?" I told her I thought it would make all the difference in the world. So perhaps if she gets that letter off immediately it may just turn the trick, all other things being equal.

In the meanwhile, Harvard Law Review has graciously accepted the idea of a review of "States' Laws" by Judge Hastie or the other two candidates I suggested, and suggests that the review should be in time for publication in the December 1951 issue. So well and good. Now to try and get Hastie to accept it [. . .].

I have just about completed the majority opinion in the case of *Dennis v. United States*, together with the concurring opinion of Justice Jackson and the two dissenting opinions of Justices Black and Douglas.[11] I have

11. In *Dennis v. United States* 341 U.S. 494 (1951) the majority held that the restraints on free speech embodied in the Smith Act were not unconstitutional. The dissenters thought they were, under the First Amendment of the Constitution. The Smith Act, which had been passed by Congress in 1940, made it an offense to

not read the copious concurring opinion of Justice Frankfurter yet. Anti-Communist though I am I must go along with the dissent in this case. The case against the constitutionality of a statute which makes "advocacy" and "teaching" of subversive doctrine and with no evidence in the record of *acts* of subversion and sabotage is very persuasive. In time you must read these decisions. This may be the kind of decision, like *Plessy v. Ferguson*, that gets stuck in the law and we have a helluva time getting rid of it. I cannot help but think the most important fight we have is the fight for freedom of speech and other civil liberties because it is through these channels we correct evils of discrimination, segregation, economic inequality and all the other dangers to our democracy. Also, what these trials and other restraints and investigations do to thoughtful citizens and young college people who dare not open their mouths to question any policy for fear it may reverberate on their jobs, their future appearance before the Character Committee, etc. etc. is tragic. [She goes on to offer concrete evidence of young lawyers who had been intimidated by the pervasive fear of what we call McCarthyism. On a more cheerful note, she mentions the fact that the University of North Carolina had admitted four African American students to its law school.]

On the sex front you may be aware of the action taken by the Bar Association of the City of New York against the nomination of Frieda Hennock as the first woman United States District judge of the New York area. She was admitted to the New York bar in 1926, the youngest woman ever to be so admitted, has been a member of a corporation firm for many years, has recently completed a two or more year stint with the Federal Communications Commission and has been very popular there. Nevertheless, the Bar Assn, headed by Whitney Seymour, has blasted her appointment as "totally unqualified" the strongest possible language which could be used [. .].[12] Mrs. Roosevelt looks wonderfully well, "was delighted to have" the clippings I sent her to Geneva because the

---

advocate, or belong to a group that advocated, the violent overthrow of the U.S. government.

12. Frieda Barkin Hennock (1904–60) was an outstanding member of the Federal Communications Commission, who, among other things, was later responsible for the creation of educational channels, which became the Public Broadcasting System. Powerful interests opposed her effort to rein in commercial broadcasting.

U.S. newspapers were so sparse. . . . [The rest of the letter deals with family news.]

Ware comments on a book called The Mark of Oppression,[13] *which Murray had recommended. In 1951, she, like many others, is clearly depressed about the state of the country. The combination of the heating up of the Cold War, the Korean War, and the campaign of intimidation launched by Joe McCarthy led many thoughtful people to despair.*

→ Vienna, Va., Sept. 10, 1951

Dear Pixie—

How goes it—in your lonely state minus Maida? And have you heard how she is getting along in Scandinavia? I got a letter from Dr. Taylor of Sarah Lawrence saying that they had an opening in a college in Wales that they were trying to get her for. I wonder if that panned out, or if she has stuck to the plan to try to finance herself at Ruskin. The Welsh college was unfamiliar to me, but might be pretty interesting.

The exchange program from there is apparently new.

My duties as an invalid-visitor-and-tender are now over, and I'm back on my own ground again. My Boston patient is flourishing [. . .]. It's certainly been a pleasure to see the process of restoration take place. I certainly hope that nothing else jumps out to lay Dad low and that he maintains his present vigor.

I read with absorption "The Mark of Oppression" and wished for you to talk it over with in detail. Several points struck me. The individual stories are all too familiar. I wish that the psychiatrist might have presented a series of his other patients. I wished that he might also have presented some "normal" representatives of the dominant group. I did not feel that he always evaluated the factor of color in relation to the other factors with complete sureness.

I think of so many white people who match some part of each story— and some who match many parts. And I think of Negro people without many of the recurrent features that appear in these stories, and with other aspects to their personalities which he does not bring out. I wish some-

13. Abram Kardiner and Lionel Ovesey, *The Mark of Oppression: A Psychological Study of the American Negro* (New York: W. W. Norton, 1951).

one would take a sample outside of New York, for all of his cases were either products of Harlem or migrants there.

But whatever modifications these further explorations would produce, this record is one to give pause. Two things especially seem to me to make the book "must" reading, the evidence on self-hate or self-depreciation, and the evidence on the price of family instability which in turn reflects self-deprecation and the evidence of the price of family instability [. . .]. The psychiatrist obviously was looking for this factor and may well have overplayed it—especially in his treatment of the middle and upper strivers for whom a class position is so important. But allowing for exaggeration and emphasis, any society which creates lack of self-respect among large segments of its citizenry is a destructive one. When I first went to Howard I was puzzled by the fact that the handicap of race did not lead to double effort as frequently among Negro students as among Jewish students. The answer certainly lies in the fact that the Jewish individual gets a chance to respect himself before he has to meet lack of respect from others.

One of the discouraging things about this book is that it makes the solutions seem so very difficult. The author concludes that cessation of oppression is the sine qua non, as indeed it is. But mere absence of oppression can't build the positive strengths that the vicious cycle here displayed has destroyed. And in our culture, which has so many characteristics that threaten the most advantaged individual, the chance for what the White House Children's Conference calls a "healthy personality" is sadly slim. I guess we just have to learn to make the most of ill-health and try to minimize the symptoms for social anti-biotics show no sign of being developed. What really seems to me most threatening is that as a people we are getting to dislike ourselves. And if our whole society is one of self-dislike what chance has the oppressed one, even without the oppression?

By way of antidote—i.e. of perspective—let me commend the other book that I bought at the same time in the south—"The Sea."[14] It was wonderful to contemplate geologic time for a bit, and the cyclical changes of seasons, and the gathering of forces of the ocean. Try it.

14. Probably this was *The Sea Around Us* by Rachel Carson, which was published by Oxford University Press in 1951.

What chance, if any, of seeing you in New Virginia? These are the golden days, and the latch string hangs out. Pauline Coggs came through (and got sick) with T & young Greg in fine spirits all.

Any job prospects for that waiting interval? And how is the law business?

Take care of yourself

Love, Skipper

P.S. Before I got this into an envelope the mail arrived with a card from Maida, mailed just as she left Sweden. It sounds as if she had a good time there and had a warm reception.

Ware had given a good deal of thought to the failings of U.S. foreign policy. Here she outlines one of her ideas for improvement.

Vienna, Virginia

December 8 [1951]

Dear Pixie,

It was good to hear from you, but bad to hear that the health was having a hard time to maintain itself against the threats of autumn colds etc. I've been sort of hoping that you might come down for a bit of a visit here, but the daily law grind makes the prospects look dubious. I sure wish that a job with regularity and a salary would come along, for you've really had enough of the hand-to-mouth life for a reasonable life time.

Your reports of Maida's dealings with the Ruskinites are delightful. I can see her taking on the prevailing attitude toward women, which irked me at Oxford nearly 30 years ago and giving it what for. The thing that used to dishearten me was the women's own expectation of inferiority which made them surprised when they achieved better academic records than the men (which they usually did, being a more rigorously selected group etc). As for the racial angle, if the U.S. was half smart it would appoint well qualified Negroes to every foreign post it could so fill to demonstrate the existence of such persons and to provide a visible refutation of the extreme Soviet propaganda. Of course, such action would make us look a lot better than we are, but the present situation is making us look lots worse. If the State Department were smart, too, it would take a heck of a lot more pains over where and how foreign visitors, especially those of color or near color went in this country and would use these thousands of visitors as leverage for various things—e.g. make hotel arrangements, and if these are refused put the hotel on a list of those for which U.S. government representatives from any agency can't collect per diem, etc. But I suppose that sort of tying together of domestic and foreign policy is too much to hope.

Anyhow, I'm glad that the Voice of America is using you, and hope they use you more. Incidentally they turned up this week to record a Howard School of Social Work Forum on "Law and Social Work: Our Common Stake in Human Rights." George Johnson and the head of the D.C. Council of Social Agencies spoke. George shone by comparison (he did a nice job).

My life goes on as usual. Gardiner is absorbed with the problems of a business to propagate and distribute the Dept. of Agriculture's latest lawn grass creation (will drive out crab grass which endears it to every suburban dweller, cemetery keeper, playing field or park custodian).

I'm struggling with preparation for a Pan American Social Work Congress that will come off in February if the Mexican government can make up its mind about sponsoring it. Thank goodness it is a clever and experienced gal from Argentina and not I who is now there trying to unscramble the political angles, bureaucratic rivalries and personality clashes. At least she is a devout Catholic who can keep up her spirits by a pilgrimage to the shrine of Our Lady of Guadeloupe.

When do we get together? My Christmas involves a trip to Brookline, to be with my parents. On the way back, I expect to put in a day at Poughkeepsie checking on my friends the Lee family.[15] At the very least

15. Ware's relationship with the Lee family, mentioned here only in passing, provides a vivid example of her conception of friendship. Dorothea Demetracopoulous, born of a Greek family in Constantinople, eventually wound up in the United States and as a student of Ware's at Vassar College. She went on to become an anthropologist, author of the much-admired *Freedom and Culture*. Returning to Vassar as a faculty member, she met and married Otis Lee, a philosopher, and had four children before Lee died prematurely. Lina Ware offered financial—as well as emotional—support and became a frequent visitor to the family in the stressful years after Otis Lee's death. She took the responsibilities of friendship very seriously. When the FBI examined Ware's life history, Dorothea Lee was among her associates described as dangerously liberal.

I'll count on catching up with you for a meal and chat en route to or from Poughkeepsie—I'll also count on seeing you when I'm in N.Y. the end of January for the meeting of the Association of Schools of Social Work. These are *at the very least*

Good luck—Skipper

In a letter dated February 17, 1952, Ware reports on a visit to Atlanta and her observation of the African American community there, which she finds full of vitality. A week or so later Murray writes about her effort to find an endocrinologist, and not long thereafter Ware sends her a check.

Murray had had high hopes for the job with the United Nations and for another, to be administered for the State Department by Cornell University, for which she was particularly well qualified.

The Cornell job, which requires a lawyer, is to be in Liberia, about which Murray knows a good deal thanks to Maida Springer's work in developing African trade unions. When she first applies for the job, Milton R. Konvitz, the Cornell recruiter, encourages her, telling her he is an admirer of States' Laws. *Then a Cornell dean, one Catherwood, apparently becomes concerned that all her references are from people who have liberal leanings and worries about the various organizations with which she had worked over the years, some of which are now labeled "subversive" by the House Committee on Un-American Activities or by McCarthy. These include the Workers Defense League and the Socialist Party. The Cornell recruiters rather ungracefully ask her to withdraw her application so that the university will not have to turn her down. In dismay she tries to mobilize all her most distinguished friends to take up her case. Many try to help, but in vain. Konvitz leaves the country and refuses to respond to her letters.*

⤜ May 10, 1952

Dear Skipper:

I don't think I have ever been so close to throwing in the sponge, as I have this week. Yesterday was the final straw. Dr. Humphrey, who wrote and told me to come in and talk with him, was forced to tell me that the present internal—financial and political—situation within the UN Secretariat makes it impossible for him to consider me for a post, although they have four professional posts vacant on their manning tables. Two must be kept unfilled for a time to absorb financial reduction of the budget. One must be filled by a French lawyer, Mrs. Boucheron's post has already been filled by a Dutch girl, and the other post is the center of controversy from an underrepresented country, which while it has not put up a candidate which meets the qualifications, nevertheless has tied up the post so that it cannot be offered to anyone else while the controversy is resolved.

With this blow, I almost canceled my luncheon appointment with Mrs. Roosevelt and made for the East River. Instead I absorbed some UN staff troubles ad nauseum until I felt better for myself and worse for them. So stay I did and had lunch with Mrs. R., who told me she read the memo on Cornell and was *absolutely furious*!. She said one has to go on, one cannot stop, no matter what. Her compassion, Eric's[16] delight with lunch, and my native toughness have made me reconsider my decision not to fight Cornell on this issue. I have no alternative but to fight. Every tack with every job I have tried has failed. Either I must lie down and the let the passerby kick me into the dirt or I must fight back. It's as basic as the law of survival.

I don't think I'll get anywhere. I think I'm a dead duck as far as Cornell is concerned, but do me one favor—read the article in the Winter, 1948 issue of Journal of Negro Education by Professor F. L. Marouse, and tell me honestly if you think they really rejected me on grounds of "bad public relations" unrelated to race [. . .].

Two revealing documents with respect to the Cornell case are in the Murray Papers. One, a six-page memorandum dated May 6, 1952, is addressed to eleven people (including Thurgood Marshall and Eleanor Roosevelt) and details the whole Cornell story step by step, as Murray interpreted it. She says that she has taken no action in the matter in the faint hope that Cornell will reconsider. The other is a letter to Milton R. Konvitz, dated May 9, 1952, in which she "respectfully requests reconsideration of my application by you, Dean Catherwood and such other members of the Cornell University as have responsibility in making a decision thereupon." Her final paragraph reads:

16. Eric Springer, son of Maida Springer, became a protégé of Murray, who encouraged him to go to law school. He did so and became a highly successful lawyer.

In view of the above considerations [she had detailed the evidence of her qualifications and loyalty] I earnestly recommend that, irrespective of what finally happens to my candidacy, you make every effort to find another qualified Negro candidate who may have this opportunity to compete on equal terms for the position for which I applied.

In the following letter, the thoughts Murray attributes to Ware are her own, though no doubt some, at least, they share. Her obsession with the Cornell case would continue for many years. She had experienced many other rebuffs in her life, but this one seems to have had a peculiar poignancy for her. "What was happening" included several things, most notably the attacks on liberals, the nomination of Dwight Eisenhower for president and Richard Nixon for vice president, and the Korean War. Murray vacillates between thinking that Cornell turned her down for her radical connections and thinking this discrimination is, as usual, on the grounds of race.

>| May 13, 1952

Dear Skipper:

I had the feeling from your recent note that you were deeply shocked and distressed by what was happening in the field of your life's effort, and that your sorrow was all the more poignant because you saw an insidious thing happening in the great tradition of academic freedom—the very bulwark of democracy. You felt that if the inquiring and insatiable mind is to be destroyed, then what is there left to fight for?

Your note, short as it was, touched me deeply, because you have been my mentor—the mind that I followed, that inspired and challenged me. You are somewhat inarticulate about things that stir you deeply and one has to be very sensitive to pick it up, but I caught it when you said, "I still haven't found adequate words with which to say what I have to say to Cornell . . . on behalf of the university tradition to which my life has been dedicated. . . ."

[Several paragraphs are devoted to reporting on what all of Murray's supporters have said in an effort to explain the Cornell rejection and to reassure her.] It took something like this to shock me out of my fear—the fear that has beset all liberals of late. I have the feeling that we will not let the termite minds of this country continue to frighten decent people into silence for fear of being smeared. When I weighed the imponderables and decided to take on Cornell, I knew that I had taken a step forward. Would prefer not to fight—but the issues are so entertwined—race, sex, liberal academic tradition—each of us must hold his ground wherever he is.

It is wonderful to have a friend like you—and I hope that someday I can make your horse a winner. [. . .] Love

Ware has her own problems in the summer of 1952 when she is denied permission to go to Chile by the International Organizations Review Board, which has the power to screen Americans working for international organizations. She comes under the board's scrutiny because she is working part time for the Pan American Union. When she writes Murray about her disappointment, the latter suggests that the problem is that Ware insists on having "chocolate friends, house guests, students and associates."

Professor Landon Storrs of the University of Houston was kind enough to share with me Ware's FBI file, which she had acquired through the Freedom of Information Act. The document makes fascinating reading partly because it reveals the methods of interrogation used by the FBI and partly because of the wildly different perceptions of Caroline Ware that it shows different people to have held. Certain informants had reported that she was a dangerous liberal who had entertained "Negroes" at her farm. Most of the people interviewed gave her high marks for character and loyalty, while a few thought she was not to be trusted, and some had wild ideas, such as that she had been part of a Communist cell; one even repeated a rumor that she was a daughter of Ella Bloor, a well-known Communist. Ware herself speculates that she has been identified partly because of her membership in the Cooperative Bookshop[17], which many people joined for the discount on books, and because of her close friend-

17. A cooperative bookstore in Washington offered a 10 percent discount to members, whereupon many readers joined to qualify. When Senator McCarthy began using the word "subversive," he applied it to members of the bookstore. The store's board of directors probably included a good many well-known liberals. People such as Lina Ware were caught in that net. I was a member, and when my husband had to undergo security clearance for a job in government, I wondered if my membership would trip him up. The FBI apparently failed to connect us, and he got his security clearance.

*ship with Dorothy Jackson, who is mistakenly rumored to be a member of
the Communist Party. True to form, Ware, disrupted though her life is,
simply turns back to work. Her letters allow the reader to go behind the
daily press and historians' accounts to see how it felt to be a loyal American accused of what amounted to treason.*

→{ Vienna, Virginia
August 16 [1952]
Dear Pauli—

How is grandmother?[18] I hope the demands of the bread and butter
law office haven't hampered her development. Any news from the Fund?

Everything chugs here. Spunky is the only pup left around, Honey and
Mirro having gone to especially nice homes. Orders for grass are reaching
disaster proportions—$1300 in one day this week. Gardiner is run ragged,
and they are cutting out their advertising for fear the supply of grass will
be exhausted. I spent last weekend with my family who are so-so, but will
go up again next week. There is still no sign of a permanent person for my
job at the Pan American Union. We are off to Puerto Rico for the first
week in September . . . [part of the letter missing]

*Like many of Adlai Stevenson's supporters, Murray believed until the last
that he would win the 1952 presidential election. Ware, who had had
doubts, made a systematic study of what could be learned about Stevenson and gradually came to support him. By the time of Eisenhower's
inauguration she is obviously very sad.*

→{ Vienna, Virginia
Jan 21, 1953
Dear Pixie—

Did you manage to stay away from a television set yesterday? Or did
you put yourself through the ordeal of contemplating the future—and
the past? If you did watch the inaugural ceremony, I'm sure you felt with
me that the one person who knew what it was all about was the rabbi and
that his prayer was the high point of the ceremony.

18. This comment refers to the book Murray had begun that would become
Proud Shoes, in which she deals with her grandmother.

Just in case you're feeling "end-of-era"-ish I'd like to share what quite unexpectedly gave me a lift. I went to the Federal Security Agency on Monday to hear Oscar Ewing's report on the international Conference of Social Work in Madras, India. It didn't turn out to be much of a report, just an account of his itinerary with some miscellaneous observations, but at the end he made his valedictory speech. It consisted in a very brief statement of some of the things achieved and some of those remaining to be done, and then a couple of verses from a poem by Kipling (of all people) that I didn't know. It's about a king who started to build a palace and found, as he dug for the foundations, the remains of a structure that had been started by some unknown hand before. On every stone were carved the words, "After me cometh a Builder; tell him I too have known." The king used these stones for his fine foundation, and built on. Then—

"When I was a King and a mason, in the open noon of my pride
They sent me a word from the darkness. They whispered and called me aside.
They said 'The end is forbidden' They said 'Thy time is fulfilled
And thy palace shall stand as the others—the spoil of a king that shall build.'
I called my men from my trenches, my quarries, my wharves and my sheers.
All I had wrought I abandoned to the faith of the faithless years.
Only I cut on the timbers, only I carved on the stone
'After me cometh a Builder' tell him. I too have known."
A good thought for these times.

Have you, by the way, seen recent articles in the New Yorker on Liberia and the Gold Coast? Both interesting in the way New Yorker articles so often are, interesting because of their carefully observed detail. The more I know about Africa the more important I think Maida's Gold Coast project is.[19] Any progress there?

At the moment I am on my way to St. Louis for the annual meeting of

19. Maida Springer had been working on developing international relationships among trade unions in the Gold Coast (later Ghana). See Yvette Richards, *Maida Springer: Pan-Africanist and International Labor Leader* (Pittsburgh: University of Pittsburgh Press, 2000).

the Council on Social Work Education. This is, as it were, a consolation prize, and not much consolation at that, for not getting off to Brazil as I had figured this Saturday. My efforts to get out of the country are surely jinxed. Since I've still been unable to get cleared to be sent on any U.S. assignment, and since the international conference I was supposed to go to last year folded, I finally decided that the only way to get anywhere was to go on my own, so I tried to work out a deal on that basis to get to a U.N. rural welfare conference in Rio de Janeiro. But after two months of messy backing and filling, even that finally fell through. After I had got my vaccination, plane reservation and travelers checks. So, that being the day before yesterday, I switched directions and came here en route.

[The rest of the letter deals with the arrival of new puppies.]

Otherwise no news.

Be good—best to Maida—

love

While Ware is writing about the inauguration and the state of the country, Murray's mind is on the closing down of her law practice, on her temporary job with the New York City Department of Social Services, and on trying to gain weight. After the trauma of the Cornell experience, she turns in a different direction. Among other things, the Cornell people questioned her loyalty; in retrospect she would say that the shock of that accusation made her think back to her remarkable family, made up entirely of loyal citizens. She thought of her grandfather who had fought for the Union and stood, as she had already said, in "proud shoes." She remembered that Stephen Vincent Benét had praised a short story she wrote about her grandfather. In her depression of spirits she decided to turn now to write a book about her family. In the midst of the welfare job she notes that the manuscript of what was to be Proud Shoes *has grown to 25,000 words, or seventy-five pages of typescript. The inauguration, she says, "passed over my head completely."*

She observes that members of the New Deal generation, viewing the election returns, are returning to private life. Her observations about the Puerto Ricans in New York must have been of great interest to Ware, whose admiration for the people with whom she worked in Puerto Rico was great. Also, her long-ago book about Greenwich Village had dealt with some of the same territory that Murray now describes to her.

388 Chauncey Street
Brooklyn 33, New York
January 21, 1953
Dear Skipper:

[She begins with a full account of the process of closing her office, moving her materials to her apartment, storing files in Maida Springer's basement, and finding a job as a social investigator with the New York Department of Social Services. She says that she was literally starving as an independent lawyer. She has a grant from the Saxton Foundation to work on the book she is writing, but the grant falls short of what she needs for ordinary living for herself and her aunts, hence the welfare job.]

The most interesting aspect of my work is my Puerto Rican clientele. I have a caseload in upper Greenwich Village, an area in which my entire caseload of some 70 or 80 families are located almost entirely on West 22nd Street between 7th and 8th Avenues. The population is almost wholly Puerto Rican, with a scattering of unattached males a number of whom are English, a few Italians and the rest Continental Americans over 65. It is an area of cheap rooming houses in which the Department of Welfare is inadvertently fattening the purses of unscrupulous landlords who buy up these old fire-and-rat traps, stick a few pieces of broken down furniture in the rooms, set up a gas plate, and rent them for $10 to $15 per room per week—and WE pay it. The victims of this exploitation are the Puerto Ricans, who have now taken the Negro's place at the bottom of the heap. They are now the porters, the elevator operators, the dishwashers and hewers of wood and drawers of water. They live in the slums in little pockets around the City. They live in casual relationships— marriage is rare—many families are mothers with several children by different fathers. Few of them speak English and their interpreters are scarcely better. So it is entirely impossible to get more understanding than the eye can see, because communication with them is inadequate.

Yet there is a shrewdness about them. As a fellow worker commented, they consider Public Assistance their No. 1 community asset and they have learned by word of mouth how to take advantage of it. The mothers never know where the deserting fathers are, they all have Clinic Cards and take full advantage of the public health facilities, they know just what to ask for. They have babies regularly—and the Department of Welfare supplies the layettes, the crib, and pays the rent for larger quarters. They move from one furnished room at exorbitant rents to another, and the Investigator spends much time tracking them down.

[She goes on to describe the way landladies take advantage of their tenants, describes one such as "a witch if ever I saw one," and comments that she has seen the same pattern among Polish Americans in Pennsylvania. She says she needs "more background into the Puerto Rican problem." After much more discussion of what she is learning, she winds up:]

I think 1953 is going to be a great year somehow. There was so much pain and frustration in 1952, the spirit could hardly withstand it, but the Saxton award had a psychological value far more than the monetary worth—it kept the spirit alive—and while I am a long way from a best seller, I think when it finally comes it will be worth reading. I want it to reflect the blend of laughter and tears which after all is the essence of every life and therefore universal.

Among my many blessings is your friendship for which I am grateful. I do hope things are going well for you and that Washington will remain an interesting Merry-go-round for you despite the travail of the past few years and the new coat of paint. I was particularly gratified to see that Mrs. Keyserling[20] was vindicated. Although we met her briefly we knew they were friends of yours and that struck home very closely to you, although you never commented upon it. After what has happened in this and other areas, particularly UN, I'm very humbly grateful to be only a little Social Investigator in the Dept. of Welfare.

→ January 31, 1953
Dear Skipper:
[Speaking of the loyalty investigations which many of her friends are experiencing, Murray assumes that she herself is also being watched.]
One feels frightened, insecure, exposed. One thinks of all the personal

---

20. Mary Dublin Keyserling, who worked in the Commerce Department, was married to President Truman's chief economic adviser, Leon Keyserling. McCarthy had accused them both of being sympathetic to Communism. Mary Keyserling had been forced to take leave from the Commerce Department, and both Keyserlings left government when Eisenhower was elected. See Landon Storrs, "Red Scare Politics and the Suppression of Popular Front Feminism: The Loyalty Investigation of Mary Dublin Keyserling," *Journal of American History* 90, no. 2 (September 2003), 491–524.

errors, the deep secrets of one's life, unrelated to political activities. One is apprehensive that all the details of one's intimate life will be spread on the record to be read, sifted, weighed, evaluated and judged by strangers.

→│ Brooklyn
Sunday May 6, 1953
Dear Skipper—
[. . .] I am overwhelmed by your response because I am still struggling with what I wanted to say in the earlier draft but had not quite said it. Your immediate response assures me that is right for the beginning of the book. Maida had the same feeling—and the two of you are my range of readers. Between you, I get all the responses, reservations, delights that I could hope for from any individual reader who would read the completed book. [She goes on to say that she is more and more convinced that *Proud Shoes* is her search for identity, a search carried on through several successive generations and crystallized and intensified in the author, who now must clearly be both narrator and participant.]

On June 16, 1953, Lina writes about her continuing problem of getting cleared to accept invitations to Latin America. The International Organizations Review Board sent her an astonishing "interrogatory." Its investigators had tracked down every organization that had come under the eye of the FBI, *or of the House Committee on Un-American Activities, or of McCarthy, with which Ware had had even the most passing connection. The board demanded an answer as to whether people whom she hardly knew were Communists or Communist sympathizers. Her answer to the interrogatory is a masterly statement of her life history. She begins with her great grandfather, details the story of the family members and includes the following paragraph:*

> *I have always found completely abhorrent the Communist regimentation of thought, the attempt to legislate scientific "truth," political and economic regimentation, the secret police and rule by fear. As an historian, I am keenly aware of the age old struggle of the human race toward ever greater opportunity for the free and full development of the human spirit [. . .].*

Her statement so impressed the board members that instead of being summoned for a hearing she was given total clearance and was able to resume her international travel. In the following letter she describes clearly the nature of her activities in one Latin American country— describing a pattern that she would follow for many years.

✈ Vienna, Virginia
Oct. 4, 1953
Dear Pauli:

I was sorry that you didn't happen to be home when my plane was grounded in N.Y. and I had tried to telephone—but was delighted to get your good report. I'm bursting to have the opportunity to read the book. If parts of it meet even your exacting standards, it should be good, and if the rest is up to what I have already seen it should be a humdinger. I wish I'd been there when you were discovering the archives. Make that return trip soon.

The news about Eric and the bar is super. Please add my congratulations, both to him and to Maida—and take a few yourself as the legal example and counselor.

I hope that I shall have the opportunity to read Maida's report. Has anything further come of her interest in the Gold Coast? The more I learn about that area, the more her idea makes sense & seems important.

My summer has been very full and my present mood is one of taking life as easy as my [illegible] commitments permit. I went to Colombia to give the intensive course in community development in Bogotá and then to repeat it in Medellín. Intensive is the word. The lectures which are being mimeographed and which I had to write because I didn't dare lecture in Spanish from notes (though I never got the whole lecture written before it was time to go to class, even though I got up at 6:00 every morning to try to finish) ran to 90 single spaced, legal sized pages, which I guess is 35–40,000 words,—a fair amount to turn out in a month in a foreign language. Just doing that would have been a full-time occupation, but that was only the beginning. I had to visit all manner of community agencies and projects to have some familiarity with the local scene in order to teach realistically, and in order to act as a consultant for the various programs and operations. Then I had to give a series of five lectures at the Inter-American Housing Center in Bogotá and to act as a consultant on their projects, and some public lectures in both cities, and to conduct a series of round tables in Bogotá for the directors of all the schools of social work and in Medellín for the various lecturers in law, medicine, sewing, nursing, morals etc. at the school there, etc. etc. At Medellín I had a very exciting seminar with a top notch group of students about their actual practice, and individual conferences with those that had particular problems, or, for example, were the first students from their cities to receive training and wanted to talk about where and how they should start as pioneers when they got home.

On top of this, word got around that a consultant was in town so all sorts of people wanted me to do something for them—the director of health and welfare for Bogotá wanted (and got) a plan for the reorganization of his department, the mayor of Medellín wanted advice on his proposed plan to set up a social service department in the municipal government and got a greatly improved plan, which he put into effect two days later. etc.

It was all very busy and friendly, and gay—they are a very cordial and warmhearted people—but it left me limp, and ready to take life easy for the coming year. A week's canoeing in the Adirondacks freshened me up, but didn't restore my zeal for work.

In Medellín one of the women who worked in the girls' residence where I lived looked, walked and gleamed wickedly so much like you that I could hardly refrain from throwing my arms about her, and I couldn't keep my eyes off her. She was a swell gal, too—but no substitute for the real Pixie. . . . Love,

Skipper

By November Murray has sent the manuscript of Proud Shoes *to Ware, and she and her close friend Helen Lockwood of the Vassar English Department are working hard to help Murray improve it. This letter is typical of the care she took with Murray's drafts, whether of letters, pamphlets, articles or—as in this case—a possible book. A careful analysis of* Proud Shoes *in light of this letter would show how much Ware and Lockwood contributed to its final form. The general comments they made on the manuscript would be useful to almost any writer. As usual, Ware is careful not to upset Murray, who could be exceedingly sensitive to criticism, though she seems to accept constructive criticism from Ware and Lockwood without dismay.*

Eric Springer tells me that, as the manuscript developed, Pauli read

parts of it aloud to his mother and himself and occasionally included his grandmother, seeking their suggestions.

→| RFD #1, Box 58
Vienna, Va.
Nov. 22, 1953
Dear Pauli,

Helen Lockwood is here this week-end and has read The Manuscript, so now I can write you with more sense of how it strikes a more outside reader. To be sure, she knows you, but isn't so identified with you, and, besides, picking manuscripts to pieces is her business. I found that she and I agreed on every point. I had already had the same reaction that she came up with, and then I agreed with some constructive suggestions of hers that I hadn't thought of.

First of all, structure: We both think you have a beautiful opening on p. 9 "If grandfather, etc.:" This is a much better opener than selling the old place for the following reasons: 1) It makes the central point of the book and sets the tone in terms of the "proud shoes," not the sense of decay, or elderly gentility; (2) it is alive; (3) it introduces grandfather, you, and the troubles right away; (4) there isn't anything interesting about selling the old place—all sorts of families all over America are doing it all the time; (5) the aunts would be much better toward the end. Though they are interesting characters against the background of the family, they are not interesting to the fresh reader when met cold in the beginning.

Both of us think that you should go from p. 15 to the chapter on the Fitzgeralds without bringing grandmother in until you have given grandfather's narrative to the point where he marries grandmother. At that point you could either go to pp. 15–19 "grandmother, as I knew her, was a plump little woman etc." and then to her background, down to her marriage, or go straight to her background and end with her as you knew her. If you want to pick up the Fitzgerald story from the grandparents' marriage, the former will get you there. If you want to pick up your story (e.g. The Well), the latter would do it.

(There are some alternatives that occur to us, the chief of which is that you start with yourself, identifying yourself as the author of *States' Laws*, and then saying something about human stories and law; or identifying yourself as an American with very American background and outlook—the American dream, and the very American heritage; or, if you want to make it grandmother's story rather than grandfather's, starting with you in school feeling resentful about the headband of the Indians, or starting with you placing the Union flag on grandfather's grave.)

Second, kind of presentation: we think it should be narrative and character throughout, avoiding editorial treatment, genealogical excursions, historical reviews, essays etc. For example, the Smiths "as history knew them" could be greatly compressed in order to get to the Smiths as grandmother knew them; the "wondering" about the manumission scene adds nothing—in fact it detracts because its speculative basis makes it not ring true and, as a result, undermines the sense of authenticity of the rest of the book. It is enough that Thomas concealed the fact that he had been a slave, and that his "freedom" was limited in the manner described on pp. 72 ff.; the post–Civil War sketch labeled "6" can be read in various versions and with various emphases, in many texts. It needn't be spelled out here. What you need to bring out is the devotion to education—since that was what your grandfather so strongly reflected—and the rest of the material on disorder and confusion etc. would come out through grandfather's missionary experience in his two ventures—where you use his diaries as [illegible]; the part about the mulattos and the South on pp. 80 ff. is interesting, relevant, and rightly placed, but a bit full and essay-like, slowing the account of the family.

These are our main comments and suggestions—apart from our general excitement to see The Book coming along. It's a wonderful and absorbing story, with some superb pages, and many more that will be as good when the unnecessary detail or comment is weeded out. I know what fun it has been to run down all the details, and you need to know them, but, knowing them, you can often leave out all except the significant detail that reveals the essence. An early draft always has stuff for the blue pencil. When you have achieved your structure and exercised a courageous blue pencil, what you have written and sketched will be a knock-out. (Where are you going to put Miss Mary's having grandfather to dinner to look him over, and your Memorial Day feelings when you tended his grave?) I could write on and on but it would be so much better to sit down with you for a long talk that I am going to wait till then. Meantime, keep her coming! It's hot. Love, Skipper

Harper comes through with a contract, and Pauli can respond to the suggestions from Lina and Helen.

✈ December 16, 1953

Dear Skipper:

Now that the excitement of getting a publisher is over and Harper's is giving me a contract, I think I can soberly turn to the job at hand and confront the problem raised by the correspondence between you and me and you and Helen on Proud Shoes. [. . .] I have rewritten the first two chapters in line with your and Helen's original suggestion and am sending them on to Helen in order that she may see the incorporation of the suggestions made.

If I can be sure that I have the start of the book right, I do not think the rest will be difficult. [She goes on at considerable length and in detail about the difficulties she is having coping with some of their suggestions, particularly with the fact that she had attributed thoughts to her great-grandfather based on her own experience of being of mixed race. On the one hand, there are many things in the manuscript that are dear to Pauli but that her critics are suggesting do not belong in the narrative. On the other hand, she feels their help is essential.] I am sure no writer was as richly blessed with the kind of supplementary cherubs I have and I want you and Helen to know how wonderful it has been for me to have you in this take-off stage. It is a great experience, and I now know that the author is having the greatest experience of all. Much love, Pixie

> *Six months later Murray was euphoric when, in May 1954, the Supreme Court handed down the Brown decision. The NAACP had made good use of the argument that Pauli herself had suggested to her law professor years earlier and had discussed with Justice Frank Murphy in 1945: that segregation was inherently unequal and therefore unconstitutional. When the decision came down, she related the event to her effort to understand her grandfather. Then she went on with a vision of what she saw as great progress yet to come. The letter, as she herself recognized, at times verges on incoherence, but it is nonetheless a vital document for the historians among us, and indeed for any person interested in the whole question of race in American life.*

→⟨ 388 Chauncey Street
Brooklyn 33, N.Y.
May 18, 1954
Dear Skipper:

How can I articulate my feelings about the Supreme Court decision? How can I describe the personal reaction to one of the biggest moments in American history—a moment in which we stood up tall, taller and more dignified than we have ever been in the Twentieth Century and said simply, "We have made a mistake and now we are correcting it!"

What more could anyone ask of one's country! Perhaps in this feeling, I find myself on a new level and can understand why there was no more bitterness among the Negroes freed from slavery than there was. Triumph can be as overwhelming as grief, and the true authorities on this decision are those who spent their youth in segregated schools of the South. And so, I can speak with authority when I say that the great inspirations in human history are not always when we avoid mistakes by a God-like wisdom, but when we suffer through our mistakes and correct them. That is what placed the Supreme Court decision on par with the other great documents of human idealism—the Magna Carta, the Declaration of Independence and the Constitution. . . .

A friend of mine who attended public schools in the North and was a fellow Civil Righter at Howard said "The Supreme Court decision was a hundred years too late. I'm now waiting for it to come up North." She, by the way, is now involved in the problem of integrated housing, the natural and normal next step [. . .].

The news of the decision came at a rather symbolic moment for me. For three days I have been trying to write from the inside the emotions and thoughts of Negroes who preferred to remain in the United States rather than settle in Liberia when they had the opportunity one hundred years ago. My character, Robert Fitzgerald, attended Ashmun Institute which was under the influence of the American Colonization Society and which looked upon the school as a recruiting center for immigrants and missionaries to Africa [. . .].

I asked myself, "what was there in America to make a self-respecting human being remain in a country where there was such disparagement on every side when he had an opportunity to migrate to a colony where the Negro was supreme?"

If I could answer this question I would have the crux of the Negro's faith in America. It was an elusive thing to write and my emotions were not at all manageable in words, particularly in trying to project the question back one hundred years ago at a time when the future was much less clear than it appears today. I have not yet written it fully and may never be able to do so, but what I had already put down on paper could well have been my comment on the Supreme Court decision. . . .

> "Was it not the *promise* of America rather than its fulfillment that had lured the people of so many nations to her shores? Should a man now leave the country of his birth because that promise had not yet been fulfilled in his case? Had not free people of color from the beginning, whenever they formally assembled to state their aspirations, pointed to the Constitution and the Declaration of Independence to support their claim to citizenship? Was not a great faith expressed in these noble documents? And would not a similar faith enable the black man to establish his birthright in time!"

While I was brooding over the above passage Aunt Sallie rushed in with the news of the Court's decision. I called Eric [Springer] who was home celebrating his twenty-fifth birthday. What a birthday present! [Murray called the Associated Press to ask if the court had indeed overruled *Plessy*. A somewhat befuddled reporter read to her from the AP wire: "unanimous decision . . . which overturned a fifty-seven year precedent. . . ."]

"Glory be! I think now maybe we have a wonderful country!" At least, Skipper, I was no more pixilated than Ralph Bunch who left his money at the cashier's window after he cashed a check, and rushed off . . . All of us unknown heroes of the struggle are busily congratulating ourselves on the lower echelons as the big guns make the statements, but last night Eric, Maida and I drank a toast to the spirit of Justice Harlan, that towering ghost that stood there over the decades silently pointing the way and giving inspiration to each new host of fighters as the vanquished turned away. . . .

Seldom are we privileged to be a personal part of such great moments of history, and it seems to me that the United States must have gone a great way toward redeeming itself and winning back many friends yesterday. It will be that much harder for Malan in South Africa.[21] His arguments will sound that much more hollow. And those who doubt the vitality of democracy will once more turn back and wonder and reflect and think perhaps . . . and once again the United States pulls off a great show . . . for while the spectacle of the McCarthy hearings rock[s] the world the Supreme Court decision comes along and pushes McCarthy right off the front page. . . .

Oh the wonder and the exasperation and the grandeur of such a people whose slow painful processes nevertheless bring democracy into greater focus than ever by letting the executioner execute himself before the greatest audience he has ever had. As much as I decry the stupid programs on T.V. and the way it dominates a household, I think it has just given the American people one of the greatest lessons in democracy that could ever have been provided had we been able to call the shots. It was also fitting that the man who defended Mrs. Annie Lee Moss against McCarthy—Hayes—should have been one of the chief attorneys on the Supreme Court decision. There is often a mystery and an irony to history that makes it more fascinating than a murder mystery—the *Progressive* issue, for example. One reads it with horror, and yet with a growing relief, for one knows that the record will catch up with the culprit sooner or later, but one could never have dreamed how it would happen . . .

[She goes on to say that she thinks the decision was all that could have been asked for, and showed great wisdom, along with a wise withholding of specific directives in order to permit participation of the principals in working out details.] A magnificent opportunity for public school teachers and so on [. . .] a feeling of relief that we are now on the right track, and even if we bumble and make mistakes, the principles are clear and are in harmony with our most time honored traditions. What a field day for educators and psychologists! What an opportunity to watch the unlearning of hatred! What a catharsis to get rid of the phantoms of fear that have kept us jumpy and nervous for centuries! [She continues in a similar vein for two more paragraphs.] How do you draw a line as to the damage done by feelings of inferiority? If you must educate the child in a non-segregated school in order to prevent psychological damage, do you

21. Afrikaner Daniel François Malan, as prime minister of South Africa (1948–54), instituted the policy of apartheid.

then commit him to segregated hospitals when he is sick, send him to segregated areas of the bus on his way to school, have him go up to the gallery when he goes to the movies, and have him drink out of a fountain marked "Colored" when he goes to the county courthouse? [. . .] once you educate the child in the fundamental processes of democracy, do you then deny him the right of choice as to the most fundamental relationship of his life—the choice of a mate? [. . .]

One other comment seems appropriate. The McCarthy record as presented in the *Progressive* dramatically illustrates how an essentially evil force spreads and corrupts each new situation it touches and how consistent is the pattern, whether the exponent be a McCarthy or a house painter or a Kremlin-sitter. Just when you think you have it put down in one area, it pops up to plague you in another . . . but the good things for which we stand also have a way of spreading . . . I should hope it would not take us as long to root out mcarthyism in its present form as it has to uproot the evils of Plessy v. Ferguson, but the verdict of yesterday gives us renewed strength for the coming struggles with mccarthy. . . .

Please forgive my ramblings . . . I'm sure I'd be just as unintelligible if I were babbling to you in person . . . but its wonderful just to babble over the right decision. . . .

Much love,

Three days later a letter from Murray on the subject of the Brown *decision appeared in the* New York Times. *But* Brown *or no, by June 1, 1954, she is back to her familiar mode of worry, this time about Maida's health. She wants Lina to invite Maida for a restorative visit at The Farm. A month later she recounts a long tale of woe about an uninvited guest who had seriously interfered with her peace of mind and then adds an even longer sad story about a conflict with the woman lawyer she had hired to help her with the revision of* States' Laws on Race and Color. *Then follows a long description of her health problems. She is struggling to finish* Proud Shoes *but takes time to write about the Oppenheimer case.[22] Then she herself winds up in Freedmen's Hospital in Washington*

22. J. Robert Oppenheimer (1904–1967), who, as director of the Los Alamos Laboratory, had done vital work in the creation of the atomic bomb, later regretted its production. In his youth he had had friends who were Communists, and in the

for what is described as "rest and recuperation." During this difficult time Ware writes several letters in quick succession. Pauli Murray's response on July 26, after going into more detail about the conflict with her assistant and her health, adds a startling bit of self-analysis.

This leads to a very incisive view of myself. Maida puts me to shame. She has educated a son, kept a household going, made a social contribution and continues to do so, with so little of the educational advantages I have had. I, with the advantage of training, etc., have never been able to carry my own financial burdens, or stick to a job for any length of time, or meet family responsibilities over a long period of time. Maida has taught me something about imposing on friends because she bends over backwards not to impose, while I have breezed cheerfully along accepting whatever was given to me, all in the name of the cause. What cause? If I fight for humanity and then am a burden and a problem to my friends and family of what ultimate good am I? If I help others at the expense of burdening my friends and family, what have I achieved? If I am not in position to keep my own health intact and carry my own weight, then how can I absorb the problems of others? [The rest of the letter details the mistake she made in taking in the uninvited guest, and describes her financial struggles.] Thanks for letting me unburden . . . I'll get over this low spell soon . . . particularly if the Dodgers keep on closing the gap between themselves and the Giants. . . .

Much love.

---

climate of the 1950s his security clearance was taken away, and thereby his part in forming science policy.

3

FAMILY

HISTORY,

GLOBAL

HISTORY

While Murray struggled to perfect her family history, Ware's life took a sudden turn when she was asked to undertake a very large, challenging responsibility as editor of the sixth volume of UNESCO's *History of Mankind: Cultural and Social Development*, which would cover the twentieth century. Her first reaction, spelled out in a long letter to Helen Lockwood, had been that she simply did not have the knowledge or skill required. Both Lockwood and Gardiner Means thought otherwise, and after much soul-searching and long discussions with both of them, she was persuaded. She assured Lockwood that she would depend heavily upon her in the process, as she indeed did.

Having agreed, Ware set forth on a systematic plan of attack. Travel, writing, and consultation in connection with the book would take up much of her time for the ensuing eleven years.

In 1954 Harper managed to secure for Murray an invitation to the MacDowell Colony, in Peterborough, New Hampshire, which afforded writers an opportunity to work on books in progress. She was able to go only after she completed the rest and recuperation from earlier surgery for which she had been admitted to the Freedmen's Hospital.

→ Vienna, Virginia
July 7, 1954
Dear Pauli

I was sorry to learn from Mil[1] when I got home tonight, that Aunt Marie's death had prevented you from completing your rest cure in the hospital (or else here) and had set you in motion for a couple of weeks to

---

1. Mil is Pauli Murray's sister, Mildred Fearing.

come. I had hoped to find you here when I got back and to have you on the farm for a few days before you go to the MacDowell community for freedom and creativity. What chance of your returning to the hospital or the farm?

Mil reports that your surgical recovery was fine but that you didn't really complete the process of rest and recuperation. You were so well started on the process when I left that I wish you had completed it for it is essential before you swing back to creative writing again.

My schedule is now as follows: This week I shall be here and into the following. I am going to Boston whatever day the following week I can persuade my father to take off for the summer cottage on Cape Cod where my sister-in-law is. He will go for the weekend anyhow. I am trying to persuade him to go early and stay late, and I will stay as long as he will. Otherwise I shall be here working. I expect Dorothy Jackson and a friend of hers from Mt. Holyoke who is going to be the new owner of black dog Susie (now that Susie's bastard pups are old enough to be separated). They should be here this week as Dorothy expected to sail for England next week, but I haven't heard definitely and Dorothy may get on the next sailing instead of this one and come later.

I shall be working on a variety of things—at the Pan American Union and getting the UNESCO history organized, chiefly. My vacation in the woods has set me up fine.

What of Maida's vacation? It would seem fine if you and she could spend a week or so at the farm before you go to MacDowell on August 1st. I hope that you don't have duties relating to Aunt Marie's affairs that will keep you in Brooklyn and make you work when you should be resting. Does Aunt Marie's departure simplify your Brooklyn household situation by making it unnecessary for Aunt Sally to go dashing off periodically? I hope it relieves you of some of the strain that you experienced between the time you were here in the spring and your return to Freedmen's.

Take care of yourself and let me know whether to expect you here in July.

Affectionately,

Skipper

Ware constantly encourages Pauli to make the most of her time at the MacDowell Colony to make progress on Proud Shoes, *and to avoid going off on other tasks. She assures her that no one in New Hampshire will be put off by her brown skin.*

→ New Virginia
August 10 [1954]
Dear Pixie:

Your report on MacDowell warms the cockles of the heart. I love to picture you in the seclusion of your study, and I know just how soggy the trail feels under foot, how the pines smell, and how birches gleam white against the intense blue sky. After all these years I can never feel that I am coming "home" to Virginia when I drive south for the pines and birches are my country.

Incidentally, don't worry about your brown face in the village. Neither local people nor summer visitors will be concerned. Someone may give you a second glance from surprise, as they give a glance to any exception to the prevailing type, whatever it may be, but not from allergy (madame author, not allurgy, though I admit that "it" fits the sense better). I have met lone brown faces all over New England in summer resorts and out, going about their business unremarked by travelers or fixtures. They (T and F) can't be more concerned than the Washingtonians in Thompson's Restaurant cafeteria where, I noticed yesterday, concern was ZERO.

The Colonists sound like an interesting and varied lot. I'm trying to place Peter Viereck[2]—guess I'll have to look him up in the Library when I'm there tomorrow so that I can visualize your sparring partner. It's good to have a combination of painters, composers and writers so that each can enjoy the other's area in an amateur way. It would be hard to relax in the evening if you all felt intensely one way or the other about Brahms.

I'm looking forward eagerly to the Lillian Smith piece. It is a fine sign that it is coming along, and good to have it as a warmer-upper to swing you into *Proud Shoes*.

My productivity isn't so great, and my "studies" not so enchanting, but I'm organizing to plunge into the 20th Century history. The Library of Congress couldn't give me an air-conditioned study, and I felt very

2. Peter Viereck (b. 1916) became a philosopher of what he considered to be true conservatism. A profile of him appeared in *The New Yorker*, October 24, 2005, 38–47.

drowsy on Deck A of the old, hot building, so I am just planning to go there to read, while I do the rest at home. For this I have converted half the guest room into a study (one bed in this room & two in Dorothy's room for double guests). As soon as the fine fluorescent lamp in which I have invested arrives it will be a very convenient and pleasant work spot. I'm getting underway slowly partly because I have some things at the Pan American Union to clear up, partly because my house has had no house-keeping from me in two years so I am trying to bring some order into it, and chiefly because this is my summer for relaxation and I am not going to put on the pressure. I have a very nice Dutch collaborator, whose first communication came yesterday. Poor man, he says he regrets the dis-tance between Amsterdam and Washington even more than I because it requires him to correspond in a language not his own. I hope an Indian will soon be found to complete the team. The author-editor of the pre-ceding volume, a Peruvian, is coming to the Univ. of Virginia as visiting professor this year, so he will soon be around and judging from the outline of his volume, he is tops. So it looks like fun.

On with your good work, and good health . . .

Skipper

Pauli often refers to the "terrors" of her life. How much the fact of be-ing "anxiety ridden" had to do with her extraordinary productivity is impossible to say. Work, protest, making friends, and writing kept the wolf at bay.

→ August 11, 1954

Dearest Skipper:

[She reports some easing of her financial problems, and says that she is working on the "Lillian Smith autobiographical piece," which had been commissioned.] I'm writing more honestly here and with less self-consciousness. I'm able to pull out the hidden fears in my own life and look at them. I've been so anxiety-ridden because of the terrors I live with all the time. Here, I find that other artists also live with terrors—like Otto Luening Music Dept. Columbia U. and composer, who grew up in rural Wisconsin, a hard, rough, outdoor life, afraid of nothing—now sighs because he is jittery about finding a snake in the woodpile on the studio porch, and admits it sadly in passing. Such sharing of common woes is so reassuring to me—you know my various terrors . . . at any rate the L.S. piece will be done with some personal satisfaction, I think . . . [She goes on to reaffirm that she had not experienced any lifted eyebrows attributable to her color.]

By this time Ware knows Murray well and, though she was as close and supportive a friend as anyone could have been, occasionally she feels the need to offer firm advice. States' Laws *here refers to a supplement to Murray's 1951 work by that name, published before the* Brown *decision, that the churchwomen responsible for the original volume had asked her to write. She has hired a young black woman lawyer to do some of the work, but there is a major misunderstanding about what the assistant is to be paid. They are soon locked in combat; Pauli is sure she is right, and the assistant is equally sure that she is.*

→ August 13 [1954]
Dear Pauli:
Since you call me "Skipper" I'll continue to offer free advice!

[She comments on Pauli's financial problems.] More important, you should not take time out now to work on *States' Laws*. The time to rewrite the introduction is after all the work on it is complete. That is always the time to rewrite an introduction to any book. *Don't have* Maida send you your notes.

Put the introduction aside, except to tell your collaborator that review of the introduction is the last step and that you are waiting to do this until everything is complete. Preferably don't touch it till you leave McDowell. If you must do it there, set the last week of your stay aside for the purpose. You are *in* your autobiography. That is what you went there to do. *Stay in it.*

I feel strongly on this and am sure I am right. It was you, not Miss Stevens, who set an early deadline for States' Laws. In any case, your illness would be reason enough for the delay. You are, of course, right about a forward-looking introduction and it will be a pleasure for you to write it when you get to it. Just let your associate finish the work and then, after MacDowell, you write your own introduction without reference to her effort.

I'm glad you have found the village as unconcerned about your complexion as I was sure they would be.

The Twentieth Century is a fine excuse to have interesting conversations with all sorts of people—or will be when people get back from vacation. I'm spending my time calling for appointments and being told that my would-be interviewee is away.

Love,
Skipper

Murray wastes no time in responding and justifying her failure to follow Ware's advice.

→ August 16, 1954
Dearest Skipper:

Just a quickie which I can allow myself, having come to the end of the draft of Lillian Smith's piece yesterday afternoon, collapsed for the evening and started what well may be the final draft early this a.m.

First, let me state that I feel privileged and very much loved to receive advice from you. It is never unsolicited, for each letter I write you invites comment on what you feel is important. Some one once said we spend half of our lives finding a friend and the other half keeping him. You are my self-appointed godmother, something we seldom have any choice in, and therefore I consider carefully every comment you make on my activities and my work. Even when I don't follow your suggestions, they have been weighed and form a part of my final choice.

I concur wholly with your feeling about the Introduction and this would have been my decision had not the following factors intervened: [She justifies in several ways her decision to work on the Introduction.] The Colony is stimulating, in that each writer exposes all other writers to his published work and point of view by means of articles, books, etc. There is an inter-office box business that is terrific. For example, my prize article, "The Origin and Development of Race Legislation in the United States," Journal of Negro Education, Winter 1953, is circulating in the library and Peter Viereck is now reading it. Peter made the challenging statement that the South is peripheral to the rest of Nation's problems and is now reading my point of view on same.

Apparently Ware had responded to a draft of the introduction to Proud
Shoes *before going off for a canoe trip. On October 15, 1954, she returns to
advice about concentration.*

I hope you can manage a work arrangement that will let you carry
forward with the momentum you have gathered and without the wear
and tear to which you have been subjected in the past.

I am still battling to get a work arrangement that will really let me
spend half time on my history instead of being encroached upon by that
half devoted to the school . . . [Her letter was interrupted by the arrival of
Hurricane Hazel.]

*The "Hazel-occasioned morning bath" mentioned in the following letter
became a favorite story: Pauli had been with Eleanor Roosevelt at Val Kill
when the hurricane cut off electric power. In order to take a morning
bath, Roosevelt had suggested that Pauli and another guest take a dip in
the swimming pool—after all, it was fall and the pool was not in use.
Unbeknown to her, some members of the Roosevelt family were in residence in a house overlooking the pool, and they were startled to see a
couple of naked women gingerly stepping into the chilly water.*

*At Howard, Pauli had written a fan letter to Lillian Smith, who
responded in kind, and a friendship developed. For a while Murray
cast Smith in a role somewhat similar to Ware's, but in the end the
friendship faded.*

[Nov 15, 1954]
Dear Pixie,
We have roared, shouted and ached with laughter over the Hazel-
occasioned morning bath, and I have regaled various friends with same—
usually going into a chain reaction of Pixie stories. Some day you must
write "My Life as a Pixie." It would make such antics as "When we were
young and gay" both tame and dull.

I was not too surprised at your publisher's reaction, for I was beginning to feel that you were off on the historian's quest rather than that
of the biographer-autobiographer. The wonderful story of your odyssey
to Delaware, Pa., Virginia, N.Car (and Massachusetts) and what the dis-
coveries meant to you as your great-grandparents and your young grand-

father came alive through the documents and places and people—that is what belongs in the book (or somewhere, maybe that article about yourself).

I hope that the revision is "coming" and that you are able to write freely now. I have the feeling that the book is going to come off in a rush at the end as you finally get to seeing right and the pieces all fall into line.

As for the trip to Georgia, it might be an interruption, but it might be the precipitant. Working with Lillian Smith, skilled craftsman that she is, might be just the thing which would get your into the groove. You'll know how you feel. But I'm not sure that it would be a delaying thing to do.

What, however, is your means of support while you finish the book. In fact, right now? I'm enclosing a little lunch money just to be sure you aren't living wholly on air. If you don't have any income in sight and if Lillian Smith is pretty sure of selling a joint piece, as she indicated in her original letter, the Georgia trip might be good from that point of view.

How complicated life is, and how difficult to have to cope with economic necessity, family relationships and the creative spirit all at once!

My creative spirit is having a tussle with the problems of how to deal in any orderly way with the complexities of the 20th century. I have been acting like a grasshopper, first on this angle, then on that—first lining up a series of pieces on Islam and then trying to figure out how to deal with nuclear physics. Right now I am trying to get the basic structure lined up so that I can go back to the parts with more idea of what fits where, it still has me baffled. I wish I had someone at hand to work with instead of a co-author in Amsterdam and another in New Delhi! And I wish the days had 48 hours or I had more speed in working.

Greetings to Maida, Smokey [Pauli's dog] and your family—
Love,
Skipper

Ware continues to have Proud Shoes *on her mind. Beyond using anecdotes to make a point, Ware often thought in concrete stories. This is a good example: as she searches for a way to help Pauli to get over whatever is slowing her progress, she reflects on her own experience of puzzling about what to do next.*

⤳ Dec. 19 [1954]

Dear Pauli:

Go immediately to the Library and read an article in *The American Scholar*, winter 1954–55 (Vol. 24, No.1) by Worth T. Hedden "On Writing the Family Novel:" The magazine came to my desk yesterday and when I spotted the article I stopped what I was doing to read it. There are only two differences between her and you. She is dealing only with the generations she actually knew, and she did not write under pressure for she resolved the problems common to you both before signing a contract. But when I came home after reading the article and found your letter, it was almost like reading the article twice over.

I was glad to have your letter for I knew that I could not assume that "no news is good news:" Bobby [Murray's niece, whose name Ware did not spell consistently] and I met at the yw cafeteria earlier in the week and agreed that we were concerned about you since silence wasn't a favorable symptom. Staring at a typewriter is a dismal occupation. Sometimes its fruitful to keep plugging—sometimes a break is indicated. I hit a stage a few weeks ago when I was going around and around in circles. Every attempt to bring order into my chaotic thoughts about the 20th century was abortive. I read volumes about this and that and only knew that the manner used by the author to present atomic physics or genetics or lord-knows-what wasn't the right manner for my job. Finally I told Gardiner that I had physical as well as mental indigestion and that I needed to recover somehow. He told me firmly to put it aside, and go busy myself at the Pan American Union or School until the week-end when he would work with me on it. Advice followed and indigestion improved. We spent the week-end batting the thing around—to no avail. But a week later a new shape began to emerge. I played with it and tried some preliminary results on Gardiner. He thought that I might have something workable. I tried it once more. Then Helen Lockwood, the good catalyst, came down and we talked our tongues off. By the time I had taken her to the airport Thursday morning, the shape of the book was clear, and by Monday night I had the outline typed and in the mail to the editor, who greeted it with enthusiasm.

It all started to clear out when Gardiner said firmly, "drop it for the moment." In this instance only a short drop was needed, but in others a longer break may be needed. That's why I thought that maybe it would be good for you to do the job with Lillian Smith—but now I learn from Helen that she is, or is about to be, abroad. Helen tried to get her to Vassar for a month or so but found she was to be away. Maybe it would be good to take off and earn your living for six months and then come back for the final spurt. Or maybe it's coming now better than you feel and the thing is to keep plugging. What bothers me is the sense of pressure. Sometimes that can be a great help when it keeps one up to a productive pitch. At other times it can be destructive. [. . .] you perform well under pressure (as I do), but when pressure becomes a source of worry and distraction rather than stimulus the result is not productive.

Anyhow, as you say, a bull session is in order and I shall be in New York for a couple of days after Christmas, seeing some people and looking in on the meeting of the American Historical Association, so let's make a date for supper on Monday, Dec. 27th

Merry Christmas to all, including Smokey

At the beginning of 1955 Murray is still in New Hampshire. In the early part of the year Ware is planning a trip to Paris to confer with her two coeditors of the UNESCO history.

In 1953 Pauli had rejoiced about having a contract with Harper, but from the following letter it appears that the editors now have told her they find what she has done to that point acceptable for publication. Certainly Lina's enthusiasm suggests that something major has occurred.

⇥ Vienna, Virginia
August 27, 1955
Dera Pixie—
Hooray Hooray, HOORAY!!

I have no words with which to communicate my joy at receiving your letter with the report from the publisher. I doubt it could have made even you feel more elated than I! WONDERFUL!

The plan for MacDowell sounds perfect. Now that you are over the hump and have this splendid word of recognition to spur and guide you, you should be able to rush (only doing each page over 5 instead of 10 times!) to a triumphant conclusion.

I am glad you have been able to make a family arrangement that lets you leave Brooklyn for a period, and I hope you will be taking off soon for MacDowell. The present momentum is to be used to the full [. . .].

Love and again hooray

Skipper

→⟨ Vienna, Virginia

October 27, 1955

Dear Pauli,

[Lina offers help with Pauli's wardrobe for the cold climate of New Hampshire.] I also got to thinking that your finances might need to be rescued while I am away and out of reach. So I went to my bank, the Vienna Trust Company, Vienna, Virginia and left five $100 checks drawn to you at the bank with instructions that they should deliver any or all of the checks at your request. So if you need to use any part of this please do.

Most of the last minute jobs are getting done. I guess we shall be ready to leave by a week from Saturday.

March on, Proud Shoes.

Love Skipper

Murray's aunt, the one who adopted her and whom she called mother, died. Along with other family members, Aunt Pauline had raised Pauli. She and her sister Sallie had lived with Pauli in New York after they retired from teaching school in North Carolina. Lina, of course, writes to Pauli upon the occasion of her aunt's death.

→⟨ October 30, 1955

[She opens with words of sympathy for Pauli's loss.] You are now free [. . .] you *must not* allow her [Aunt Sallie] to take it for granted that your life is to be led for her and in terms of her needs. Your life must now be led in terms of your own needs . . . [She wants Murray to go to Vassar College to see Lillian Smith and Helen Lockwood. A year earlier she had told Helen that it made her happy that her closest friend was getting to know Pauli better, adding "she is someone very special."]

Ware had spelled out the whole story of her encounter with the International Organizations Review Board in a letter to Helen Lockwood, one of the four people to whom she had confided the fact that she was under examination. Gardiner and Murray, along with the dean of Ware's school, were the others. Only now has she gotten around to telling Pauli about the outcome. Perhaps she was sensitive to the fact that Pauli's own problems with loyalty investigations were less tractable since she could not undo her long-ago association with the Lovestone faction in the American Communist Party or her membership in the Socialist Party.[3]

✈ In the sky over the California desert
November 5, 1955
Dear Pauli,

I hope by the time this reaches MacDowell it will find you already there, after a very refreshing time with Lillian Smith and Helen. I am torn between wanting you to stay and savor their company, and wanting you to feel like getting on with the book.

With much pulling and hauling, we managed to get off at the crack of dawn this morning with most of the things that needed doing done. [She apologizes for not sending another warm suit as she had intended.] I did get the additional $200 left for you at the bank, and I told Mrs. Coates that there was a slim possibility that you might come down and occupy the house if you got put out at Peterborough.

I was overjoyed to learn of Bobbie's reinstatement. Let us hope that this is the last time that she is a "case." Incidentally, I didn't report to you that the International Organizations Loyalty Review Board finally got around to clearing me. They called me in June—more than a year after I sent in the interrogatory—saying they wanted to see me, but I was leaving for Central America that night. Then in August they called to say that they had set a hearing date in September. I asked the secretary of the Board, who called me, what more they wanted to know than I had set forth, and asked if I could come down and consult the examiner so that I could come to the hearing prepared with what they wanted, as I couldn't see what more there was to say than I had said in the interrogatory unless they had additional charges. He said he would arrange for me to see the examiner, but when I called to ask when he said that he had reread my

---

3. Jay Lovestone (1897–1990) was, and remains, a controversial figure who broke away from the American Communist Party. For a while he worked with the American Federation of Labor, and Murray had known him then.

interrogatory and was "impressed" and had given it to his chairman (now) for reconsideration and had called off the hearing. He said that the decision to have the hearing was made over a year ago when the interrogatory was received and the Board was new. "They have learned a bit since then," he observed. In due course, a couple of weeks ago, along came a copy of the clearance. At last—and, I am glad to say, without the necessity of a hearing and its attendant publicity. Actually, you, Helen Lockwood, Gardiner, and Dean Lindsay are the only people who even know about the interrogatory, apart from the lawyers whom I consulted. I am glad that the Board is "learning"!

I enclose my itinerary, with the places indicated where I expect to pick up mail. Of course, there may be plenty of changes en route. I also return the material on Bobbie. Love, Skipper

By December of 1955 the board of the MacDowell Colony has extended Murray's scholarship and she is finishing Proud Shoes. *Though Lina as usual urges her to concentrate on her writing, Pauli is somewhat distracted by her interest in what would become Stevenson's second campaign for the presidency. She notes Rosa Parks's refusal to move to the back of the bus in Montgomery and other post-*Brown *signs of a burgeoning civil rights movement.*

→{ December 10, 1955
Dearest Skipper:
[. . .] Proud Shoes, like a veteran from the wars, is hobbling along home. Have rewritten one chapter and completed four new chaps since my return from New York and end is definitely in sight—word limit almost exceeded. It comes slowly, for I must absorb both the emotional and biographical experience of Mother's passing—but it is coming surely I think. This place has great healing in it—it's only disadvantage being that perhaps I've been too much alone at a time when I should have been around people who know me well. [She thanks Lina for providing the money to tide her over while she struggles with settling her aunt's estate, such as it was.] At home we've been having a merry time of it. Stevenson has declared himself, I've joined his committee by mail, Mrs. R. stole the show at the AFL-CIO convention, Maida tells me, by being at her best—

warm vibrant and telling all she learned about the labor movement from Rose Schneiderman, then calling Rose to the platform. Rose later said that had she had a bad heart she would have had heart failure then and there. Stevenson has been getting mild attacks from G. Mennon Wms. gov. of Michigan and [Averell] Harriman, gov. of NY, but he has strong support from Lehman, Mrs. R. and the Negro vote trend toward Democratic party has risen several percent since 1951 according to the Gallup poll. We're having warfare in the south, more mysterious killings of NAACP local presidents, 2,000 Georgia Tech students demonstrating at Gov. of Georgia's request that they cancel Sugar Bowl game against U. of Pitt because of presence of Negro on latter and non-segregation in seats to be sold by Pitt—Gov. has to back down—this game allowed but no future games where Negroes or non-segregation present—more demonstrations by other Georgia college students affected by Bd of Regents rule; thousands of Montgomery, Ala. Negroes boycotting city busses because Negro woman arrested and convicted when she refused to move to rear; ICC [Interstate Commerce Commission] ruling that all railroads (and bus lines I think) desegregate interstate passengers by Jan. 10; Edwin White, member of Miss. Legis. letter in Dec. 1 *Times* that real reason South won't give up segregation is that "the races are friendly to one another" and miscegenation and misbreed population is inevitable in absence of segregation which will lead to "death of race which brought civilization to the world" through degeneracy. Letters must be pouring into Times in refutation; 2 appeared yesterday, one from Mississippi. Mine will doubtless be suppressed! But these are the growing pains of democracy. Oh yes, Va. legislature trying to evade Supr. Court decision by voting state funds in aid of private schools where white people can send their children to avoid desegregation. Those astute legislatures have never heard of the 14th amendment applying to *all* forms of State Action. Well, let them squirm. . . . I love the ice and snow here. We've had it for two weeks and normal temperature is 8 and 10 above most of the time. Deer season has everyone jittery. Local hunter shot through local farmer's living room, missing his wife by inches. Everything at the Colony posted, including Smokie who wears a bright red sash and bow, for hunters will shoot at anything moving. My red pants are wonderful, and I live in the red comforter, completely forsaking my red flannel robe. The comforter is so wonderful for reading in bed. Much love to Gardiner. [She goes into detail about the factions in New York that are split between Stevenson and Harriman, and reports the criticism that Stevenson is saying nothing about what is going on in the South.] We're to be open all winter here at MacDowell and I have another extension to Jan. 1. Should be close to the end by that time. Love

> On June 4, 1956, Ware writes another letter of condolence upon the death of Murray's remaining aunt, Sallie. On June 10 she writes about her pleasure on seeing Harper announcing Proud Shoes, and says Murray was right to take a job with the Tuberculosis Association. Meantime Murray has told her that she cannot resist having another round in support of Adlai Stevenson's second campaign for the presidency.
>
> Peggy McIntosh, Lina's niece, who admired her greatly, said she had never known anyone who worked as efficiently. The following letter provides an example of that efficiency as her father's death takes her yet again to Boston.

✈ October 2, 1956
Dear Pauli—
I can't think of a better spot for you to be in, after your long period of book-immolation than in the midst of the Stevenson campaign. In fact it's the perfect road to refreshing activity [. . .]. (I assume that you have rested up a bit [and are] reestablishing your old contacts and the period of extraversion that you rate after the long stretch of introversion that the book exacted. More power to you. Is Lile Carter also on the paid staff? He promised his wife not to load himself with volunteer activity, when he left here, so I'm wondering whether he has already slid back on that resolve, or whether this is a job [. . .].

I got back here a couple of days ago after struggling with the contents of the family house. I left my brother and sister-in-law to finish the job when it seemed that they would be able to work better with me out of the way after I had completed the part of the job for which I was responsible. I resumed work and trust that I can stick to it and maintain a reasonably high level of productivity from now on. I managed to work well the first week in Brookline, but not thereafter, even when there was nothing for me to do and the periods of sitting with my father were brief. Now I shall be able to drive ahead, with the worry about Dad over. We are so happy that he could live with vigor to the end and then could go quickly, as he wished, that we have no regrets—only thankfulness.

The temptation that I have to resist is to drop my work and plunge into the campaign. I'll have to limit myself to contributing my vote and my money and let you expend the energy for the two of us.

Love, Skipper

P.s. I'll be in N.Y. for a meeting on Oct. 9th and will try to reach you by phone.

On October 30, 1956, Lina writes asking for six copies of Proud Shoes *to spread around.*

Once again General Eisenhower overwhelmed Adlai Stevenson at the polls. The Suez Crisis came at a critical time, and the "don't rock the boat" argument could be made to support Eisenhower. As she had four years earlier, Pauli cherished hope for a Stevenson victory until the end.

Lloyd Garrison had long been one of Murray's consistent supporters. He had tried for some time to find a place for her in the law firm in which he was a partner. Now there is another attempt.

+ November 7, 1956

Dearest Skipper

Our defeat is still too new and too overwhelming for me to make any intelligent comment. Enclosed are a few comments from the New York Times and the New York Post.

Balloting on the *Proud Shoes* front has been a little more satisfying. A radio station in Thibodeaux, La. did a several-minute review of the book October 18th. The announcer [. . .] gave a good summary of the book, said that one might question battle information but could not certainly question the integrity of the book, that it was a timely document, and some of the views expressed by P.M. would be good for both races. In Akron, Ohio paper gives a rave review, calling P.S. an amazing book, written with eloquence, understanding, etc. and candor. Will save all of these for a scrapbook record for you to read at our next meeting.

Lloyd Garrison has suggested a proposition which sounds interesting.

His firm[4] has need of a librarian—not entirely full-time—but he thinks if I am interested, I might be able to do my writing on the side, or to take a fling at briefs, if they had need of such, or even to do a little practice. The salary would be modest but enough to live on—around $5000 and the hours would amount to about four days per week. I told him I was interested, that I recognized the prestige value of being associated with his firm in any connection, and that this might be an opening wedge, since earlier in the summer they rejected me as a lawyer-associate in spite of Lloyd plugging hard for me. Didn't think a lawyer who had only a one-man office practice experience was quite experienced enough for a good position in their firm, and felt that my age and other talents made me overqualified for a beginner's salary. Lloyd will have some definite information on this suggestion by tomorrow or next day. I think it might be a good move at this time. Let me have your comment. If it jells, it may be immediate which means I won't have much time to rest before going to work—but the work won't be exhaustive so I can catch my breath while earning a living.

Much love—and warmest regards to all thereabouts.

On November, 10, 1956, Ware writes that the Lloyd Garrison job sounds like a good move. She is happy that Wayne Morse has been reelected to the Senate from Oregon and that there would be an Indian from California in Congress.

⇥ December 2, 1956

Dearest Skipper:

There is so much to report, I hardly know where to begin. I almost expected a gentle chiding from you that I upped and rushed into work before allowing time for rest from the campaign, but in view of the importance of the challenge and the economic pressures, it seemed justified. [. . .] The firm has 53 attorneys—20 partners and 33 associates. There are five women among the "brethren"—one partner and one associate in the Washington office (the partner appears to be Carolyn E. Agger) and three associates in the New York office of which I am one. There is

4. Garrison was a partner in one of New York's best-known law firms, Paul, Weiss, Rifkind, Wharton, and Garrison.

presently one Negro attorney in the firm—your humble servant. The problem is, of course, standards, law school affiliations, Law Review status, etc., and promise—whether an associate appears to have the kind of future which will permit him to be invited to become a member of the firm.

This is, without question, my greatest challenge and I am fully aware of the rust on my legal equipment and the lack of experience and finesse of one who is veteran of a one-man law office. I am not panicky—I grasp legal problems quickly—but I am so very ignorant that I consider myself an apprentice and am trying to forget everything I learned in private practice on my own except how to use the law library. I shall probably make it my special business to become a crack corporation lawyer, familiar with problems of taxation, estate matters and all the areas which I pooh poohed at Howard U. Law School. [She goes into detail about individuals and individual cases. She describes the staff luncheons, and some cases discussed at those luncheons.]

Lloyd Garrison goes around beaming like a proud papa, yet for all my levity about this I know how serious is the business of the year ahead. I rationalize that I have earned my right to be delivered from the civil rights struggle long enough to become a top notch lawyer in my own right—or what is more honest to give the profession a real try, at least as conscientious a try as I gave Proud Shoes. The law—as it is practiced in this firm—will not permit a dual interest, and that is as it should be. I have much to learn and it is an atmosphere in which I will receive constant friendly stimulation. If I can do well here, it will mean much to those who come behind me, particularly the gals in the profession.

Of course all this opportunity is not without its limitations. Our senior partner, former Judge Sy Rifkind, in charge of litigation is said not to have a woman near litigation, that he would not even consider a woman as his law clerk. Being middle-aged and not possessed of the fire of youth, I have become more wily. No crusade is in order—just quiet outstanding work that comes to his attention in written memoranda, briefs, discussions. It will be worth the extra effort and hope for excellence just to see his prejudices bend a little if not weaken and fall of their own weight. So much for the law at this point. [She goes on to describe a gathering at Morgan State College in honor of Proud Shoes and its author, to which nearly every member of her family had come. She refers to a rift in the family that had led to a lawsuit, and saw this occasion as healing the wounds. She next describes taking her niece Rosita to meet Mrs. Roosevelt, and then goes on to a detailed report of reviews of *Proud Shoes*. For the moment she has landed on her feet.]

In an undated letter, presumably written sometime in 1957, Ware encourages Murray about the new job. Judging by Murray's journal, she is doing much more than being a librarian. She describes writing briefs that were sternly critiqued by a partner who had been assigned as her mentor. She works very hard to live up to the standards of the firm.

A year later Pauli had, apparently, written for advice when Paul, Weiss offered her a chance to be—presumably permanently—their person to do small claims. She does not find such an offer exactly flattering, but Lina tries to see the best side of it.

→ October 17 [1958]
Dear Pauli:

[. . .] Your report on the situation at the office is reassuring. It means, in essence, that you can have an interesting, if not world-shaking, job that offers security for as long as you want it, which is good. It means that you have made the grade in a solid way that makes the firm ready to place a continuing responsibility in your hands. From their point of view you are a real 'find' if you will play. I can see that small claims don't fit the young and ambitious, from the firm's point of view, even though the y. & a. would grab them eagerly for their educational and experience value, for the y.& a. would soon become restless and move off to something else leaving the job of breaking someone else in on small claims to be done all over again. They are an important aspect of the firm's work—for public relations, for completeness of service, etc. and must be done well, but they are a nuisance to those who are hooking and playing the whopping big fish. Then in comes P.M. and they try her out and find her competent, reliable, independent—just what the doctor ordered for that small claims department that doesn't fit either y & a or the sport fishermen (big game hunters). Made!

For you, I think it has real merit. When you went in to the firm, you had to drive yourself like fury, and it was exciting and challenging and grueling, and you made the grade. But that's not a pace to be kept up indefinitely. And you're in a fiercely competitive milieu where you can't very well play for the really big stakes. To come through to a good niche of your own that is manageable, responsible, has scope, and lets you get around inside instead of being stuck in a corner doing tax returns, or estates is, in my reckoning, damn good. [She goes on in the same vein, pointing out that such a job might allow breathing space for creative writing. She reports that one chapter of her World History has gone to Paris.]

Love

Skipper

Pauli's attachment to the firm led to a most important friendship with Irene Barlow, the manager who kept this group of high-powered lawyers in some semblance of order. Renee, as she was called, had been born in England but was brought to the United States by her mother, who had been deserted by her husband. She raised Renee and her other children single-handedly, and by the time Renee and Pauli became friends "Jenny Wren," as she was called, was living with her daughter. Murray and Barlow's friendship was built on many things, but not least their shared commitment to the Episcopal Church, in which both were very active. The two women took holidays together and wrote when they were apart. Before long Renee becomes yet another Ware-Means protégé. She will visit The Farm, and she and Pauli will remain close for sixteen years, until Renee's death in 1973.

In 1958 and 1959 the correspondence slows. Lina was in the midst of the very hard work required by her commitment to the UNESCO book, and Pauli was caught up in the buzz following the publication of Proud Shoes.

On May 13, 1959, Murray writes that she has had a conference with Francis X. Sutton of the Ford Foundation and found him much interested in the question of legal education in Ghana.

As the 1950s draw to a close, Ware reflects with profound pessimism on developments in American society. On November 5, 1959, she writes:

[. . .] The question of whether a purposeless, soft, fuzzy, mercenary society such as ours can stand up to the purposeful, disciplined people like the Russians is 'No.' The basic situation seems to me a very serious one. By handing our society over to Madison Avenue we are selling our birthright of integrity and human worth for a mess of phoney pottage (remember that little dog checkers and the Republican cloth coat?) We'll go on voting down bond issues for schools, and the streets will get fuller of kids with no sense of values, out for kicks, and we'll have even less power of discrimination and capacity to resist the next wave of McCarthyism when it comes along. [. . .]

Caroline Ware as an undergraduate at Vassar.
Courtesy of Special Collections, Vassar College Libraries.

Gardiner Means and Caroline Ware in their youth.
Courtesy of Peggy McIntosh.

*Pauli Murray as an
undergraduate at Howard
University. Courtesy of
the Schlesinger Library on
the History of Women in
America, Radcliffe Institute
for Advanced Study,
Harvard University.*

*Passport photograph of
Murray taken for her
trip to Ghana in 1960.
Courtesy of the Schlesinger
Library on the History
of Women in America,
Radcliffe Institute for
Advanced Study, Harvard
University.*

Ware at work in the Office of Price Administration's consumer relations division. Courtesy of the Franklin D. Roosevelt Library, Hyde Park, New York.

Ware listening intently, as was her custom. Courtesy of Peggy McIntosh.

Lina and Pauli in conversation with an unidentified person at The Farm, spring 1978. Courtesy of the Schlesinger Library on the History of Women in America, Radcliffe Institute for Advanced Study, Harvard University.

Gardiner and Lina before the stone fireplace at The Farm "given to Pauli with love Skipper and Gardiner . . . July 18, 1980." Courtesy of the Schlesinger Library on the History of Women in America, Radcliffe Institute for Advanced Study, Harvard University.

Pauli on the day she celebrated her first Eucharist, at the Chapel of the Cross in Chapel Hill, North Carolina—the church where her grandmother had been baptized as a slave child. Courtesy of Susan Mullally.

✈ 4

GHANA,

UNESCO, AND

BEYOND

By 1959 Pauli Murray was once again restless. Maida Springer, who had had a long association with what had been the Gold Coast and was, as of 1957, the newly independent nation of Ghana, sent her an advertisement for a lawyer who could teach in the new University of Ghana Law School. Murray applied for the job, and when the Ghanian government expressed interest but said it had few resources, she negotiated an agreement with the Ford Foundation for a grant that would enable her to accept the opportunity. Lloyd Garrison helped arrange for some refresher lessons at the Columbia University Law School, and her friends at the law firm rounded up books to donate. In January of 1960, thanks to a loan from Ware, she set sail on a Norwegian freighter, along with dog and books and things she might need. This adventure led to a flurry of letters. Ware realized that this move was a major undertaking for a person who had never before left the country and who had very little knowledge of the realities of life in a newly freed African country. As a consequence she sent off letter after letter, beginning even before the ship arrived in Africa.

Her concern was more than justified. Murray's first contact with Ghana was traumatic. She was almost immediately homesick, the tropics were bad for her collection of health problems, and she suffered from culture shock. She was dismayed by the accommodations at first provided by the university. She has been warned that they would not be luxurious, but apparently the reality was a shock. In her journal she writes that she had expected people to make more fuss over her and to provide more gracious living. For a while she found it impossible to write letters, yet in her journal she castigates friends at home who fail to write as often as she would like.

After the initial adjustment, Murray worked hard at teaching and at learning about Ghana, but she was always on the edge of depression. When the first shocks subsided a bit, she began writing fairly positive letters to Ware and other friends, while at the same time pouring out her unhappiness in journal notes. As long as Murray was in Ghana, Ware kept up a steady stream of encouraging notes.

On February 3, 1960, having just seen Pauli off on the freighter, Lina writes urging her to see this assignment as a great adventure. Again on February 11, an enthusiastic letter says that she is expecting a visit from Pauli's two closest friends, Maida Springer and Renee Barlow. Six days after that an air letter goes off to Monrovia, Liberia, where the freighter is to land, and then another, with notes from Gardiner, Mary Gresham, Renee Barlow, and Helen Lockwood, as well as Ware.

✦ March 11, 1960

[. . .] One observation and suggestion: you are an American. Period. Not a Negro American, or an American Negro, or an Afro-American or anything else with an adjective or a hyphen. You can do more to clarify yourself and to clarify the USA and further relationships all the way around by maintaining a firmly American—period—stance. [. . .][1]

She adds that she and Gardiner have been invited to the Salzburg Seminar in Austria. Pauli responds that she has walked into a challenging situation since the Ghanians are about to write a constitution. At this point Ware's letters begin to indicate that her enormous undertaking for UNESCO *is drawing to a close. A paragraph in the Author/Editors' Preface to the volume shows just how challenging the project had been:*

This volume, which deals with the twentieth century must, by the nature of the subject, be more tentative and more varied in the range of materials than those which treat earlier periods. For it has been written in the midst of the events and trends to which it refers and it

1. Kevin K. Gaines devotes chapter 4 of his *American Africans in Ghana: Black Expatriates and the Civil Rights Era* (Chapel Hill: University of North Carolina Press, 2006) to Pauli Murray and especially her reaction to the Congo Crisis. He is critical of Murray's approach to Africa.

*deals with the many facets of contemporary life for which only the
perspective of time can provide a fully integrated view. The material
for many parts of the volume had to be freshly synthesized, since no
comprehensive studies were available on which we could rely. Much,
in fact, had to be drawn from the direct experience of living people
rather than from written sources.[2]*

By spring Murray had begun to write letters again.

✈ Paris

April 16, 1960

Dear Pixie:

It was fun to get your letter—very fast—reporting the detail of your
bout with illness and mis-diagnosis and also to know that you were feeling
that you were swinging into stride with the local situation—psychologically. I had a number of observations to make on your bulletin in
which you related to the emerging pattern of authoritarian government—
which I read on the plane en route to Paris—but got sidetracked by the
health problems and guess the remarks are irrelevant now.

It does occur to me however that of your two assignments, the Law
Review and Constitutional Law, the Review is by far the most important.
This can be a truly dandy creative activity, the first forum for the discussion of African law. I can't imagine a more far reaching and challenging
assignment and one which calls for your best talents and is wholly in line
with what you have to offer. I could wish you had not been given the
constitutional law assignment because it can get you into such precarious
areas that it could sap your energy for other things and also could have
repercussions that might reduce the effectiveness of your Review. You will
doubtless find how to avoid these possible dangers. If your assignment is
clearly comparative constitutional law, it could be fun. If it is primarily
the legal implications of the Ghana constitution it could be less interesting and more explosive (unless you did it in a dull and routine fashion
which of course you would not.)

I have found here [. . .] a UNESCO publication on Social Implications of
Industrialization and Urbanization South of the Sahara. It is a fat volume

2. Caroline F. Ware, K. M. Pannikar, and J. M. Romein, *History of Mankind: Social
and Cultural Development.* Vol. VI, *The Twentieth Century* (London, 1966), xi.

which assembles the best [illegible] plus a lot of national reports of conferences sponsored by UNESCO—the one a couple of years ago. I'll send it to you when I leave here after using it myself.

My two colleagues left today after winding up our work session in fine order. The Indian's parting comment was "I feel well satisfied with the book"—and the Dutchman agreed "This is very gratifying to me." We have a problem of publication as perhaps I wrote you, because one of the volumes is fat and has to be redone and the contract with the publisher calls for simultaneous publication of all [. . .] so I have a mopping up operation before I can go home, and some further mopping up on bibliography, charts and a bit of checking after I get home. But the pressure is off, Hooray! [. . .]

I'll be here for two weeks more, perhaps less if I work fast. Then home as a free woman! Love, Skipper

Ware had put a great deal of thought into the problems of newly independent countries. She and Gardiner talked a great deal about major issues of foreign policy as well as those of domestic economic and social policy. Her mind was clear, and her analytical abilities were unusually good. In the following letter she is in her teacherly mode.

Dorothy Jackson had done graduate work under Lina's direction at American University and earned a Ph.D. at Yale. She is now working in England.

⤴ Paris-Still
April 27, 1960
Dear Pixie,

Your wonderful letter on your visit to Nisalene has come and been relished by me and Dorothy Jackson, who has come over to spend some days and give me a bit of help in Paris, and has been sent on to Gardiner and Mary [Gresham]. What a delightful experience and how reliable your instinct! This is one of the things that I would be quite sure about— that you would make the right responses and maximize the interchange in any social situation.

I was interested in what you said about the young man who took you to the village. I am sure that you will find yourself working with many like him. He faces the problems of anyone in a state of cultural transition. It is not at all surprising to me that he stayed in his city clothes. For you to don kente was an act of courtesy and appreciation; on him it would have implied acceptance of certain authority and rigidity from which he is freeing himself—and must free himself. I am reminded of a story which I heard Lillian Wald tell of the children of immigrants on the East Side who insisted that their parents use dime store aluminum pots and get rid of the "old world" brasses that they had brought with them. She at Henry Street had always offered to the parents that she would keep any of the brasses they cherished and did not want to sell, and she gave them an honored place around the House. She said that one of her greatest satisfactions had been to be able to give these brasses back to the grandchildren who were sure enough of themselves to be able to appreciate their grandparents things and to fit them into their own lives without being threatened by them.

I am sure there are few problems more central to African development than the adaptation between the chiefs and their role and the new institutions of the new states. As you say, the chief and his elders and ceremonials are to you people who have not had to outlive the indignity of slavery, and it is a heartening experience to meet them, to recognize their dignity and a kind of wisdom—At the same time they are the instruments of a social order that is in the process of change, and they may be obstructions to needed change. It will not be easy for Ghana—or any other country— to make full use of the positive qualities the chiefs have to offer without increasing the difficulties which their power and traditional practices may entail. The trick may lie in the skill with which dignity and ceremony can be divorced from effective power. One of the geniuses of the British is their capacity to take an outworn institution and turn it into an ornament—their Lord Mayors with gold braid and mace (and no power), their royalty in fact. In India at the time of independence the question was whether the princes would go along with a united India or the country would fall apart. A few of the leading maharajas were persuaded to settle for their titles and their wealth and to let go of their power, and the leadership was persuaded that the price was cheap for unity and effective power, however much they might have liked to get rid of the titles along with caste & untouchability, and to have the very considerable wealth which the maharajas commanded.

I'm sure your future bulletins will be full of aspects of this problem as you go along. I think that it is especially fine that you had this rich, warm, moving eastern experience early in your stay.

As you know I am still here in Paris plugging away. Oh for my good Vienna typist who knows how to get out the work! The mechanics of getting the corrections incorporated and manuscript prepared are dragging along with an English typist who has a bad back & therefore finds everything to do except stay at the typewriter, and a nervous French girl who disappears home with an armful of work, and I never know when she will reappear with it done. Dorothy Jackson [. . .] is helping with the checking etc. which is pleasant and relieves the tedium. I fear I shall be here for another couple of weeks, as the executive committee of our commission is meeting and it seems smart for me to be around even if I could get the ms. done earlier, which I can't. Paris is very chilly, but is still a pleasure to the eye.

The enclosed from an English paper will interest you. love, Skipper

Pauli replies promptly

➤ [Accra]
Tuesday, May 3, 1960
Dearest Skipper:

I'm delighted to know you caught up with Dorothy Jackson [. . .] I was particularly glad to receive your comments on the Easter in Ghana bulletin [. . .] I was glad to have your historical analysis which sets it in perspective for me, particularly comments about how the British have turned institutions of power into ornaments. This, of course, could be the answer for the newly emerging countries [. . .] the dilemma of African leaders—how to modernize and industrialize without sacrificing the values inherent in the tribal society. [She goes on to describe in detail her review of some proposed legislation.] This review and comment on legislation (proposed) is apparently one of our functions and will challenge me considerably, since I am expected to know what the U.S. method is in such cases. [. . .] Except for occasional homesickness at odd hours, I am in good shape.

You'll be pleased to know that for about a month Yaro [her houseman] has been attending evening Mass Education Class and the other day he brought me his Arithmetic Reader and writing book. He can write his name: "Mr. Aredi (Yaro is a nickname, I discover) Frafra" and he is actually reading. I'm so pleased, and so is he. . . .

I know your dilemma about typists—it seems once we leave the U.S. competent, fast typists disappear in thin air. The clerical problem here is unmentionable—in fact the administrative area leaves much to be desired. One bogs down in it like Brer Rabbit in the Tar Baby story and the only thing to do is to be patient and take three days to do something that one normally does in a few hours.

[. . .] To repeat [. . .] I intend to teach a course in comparative Constitutional Law which should be lively and interesting theoretically. The great problem will be the lack of background of the students. Only 7 out of 50 passed the Part I Bar Review exam given by the Law School recently. They are working students without undergraduate degrees or disciplines. Their experience is limited and they experience difficulty with complicated concepts in the English language, I am sure. Here's hoping for the best.

Much love and success in your mopping up efforts.

By September Ware has spent time on Yellow Head Island, the place she and Gardiner had recently acquired on the coast of Maine, and now writes from Virginia. Ever the teacher, she is especially encouraging to Pauli in her endeavor to teach these most unusual law students. It is again clear that she has thought a great deal about the problems of newly independent countries as well as about the real meaning of socialism.

⇥ September 17, 1960
Dear Pixie,

I have been very remiss in my letter-writing—for which apologies herewith. While on vacation—that wonderful coast of Maine that must be on your itinerary when you come home—I got as far as getting an airmail letter at the local P.O. when we paddled ashore, but we put to sea again in the canoe before I got the letter written—and then it was time to drive the long Journey home just in time to make the first faculty meeting at school (where I am putting in this semester to hold the job for Kathleen in February as I think I told you), followed by the usual scramble of planning, registration, arranging with the agencies where students will do field work, setting up courses etc. before classes start this coming week. And my guest bed or beds have been occupied on one night stands every other night since we got home—last night it was Maida on the eve of taking off for Nigeria and points adjacent. Her luggage included a couple of tiny tot staplers, the Brahms Double Concerto, and a package of canine vitamins for Smokey, which he is allowed to share with God Bless if he desires. [God Bless was the dog belonging to Pauli's houseman.]

Jim Nabrit made his bow as Howard's new president at convocation this week and was reported to have given a strong, forward looking speech. I didn't hear it by reason of the state of my academic hood, in tatters after long years of use.

Yesterday Nabrit came to the opening meeting of the School of Social Work. I took him down to the meeting room and he immediately asked "Have you heard from Pauli?" I told him you had started your constitutional law lectures and had responsibility for developing a law review. He then promptly used you in his speech to tell the students to set their sights high for who knows where they will be or what they will be doing five years from now. He sent you his greetings and said that I must be sure to let you know he was asking about you.

I shall be most eager to see the material that you are preparing for your course. What sort of response are you getting from your students? Are you far enough along with them to know whether you can arouse discussion and inquiry as well as questions of content? I think that your method of building up notes and illustrative material sounds excellent, as if the result should be something very reusable in the future—the foundation for developing a body of material.

What of the Law Review? Has there been a beginning of thinking and work toward the establishment of a Review? You said earlier that it was to be one of your responsibilities, and it seems to me, from this distance, as the most potentially exciting of all your duties and opportunities.

The enclosed clipping is from a recent issue of the Afro. A friend of Mary's caught it and Mary passed it on to me. I have said all along that one day somebody is going to "discover" *Proud Shoes* in a big way. To have it pop up like this indicates that the possibility is real.

On your inquiry about good material on the American economy, I will put my mind on locating sound and intelligible and usable stuff and let you know or send on what I come up with. It is certainly desirable that a reasonably accurate and understandable picture of that economy should reach other countries. I don't know what the USIS [United States Information Service] library may have. But material from the 1930s could be rather out of date in its emphases.

The newly developing countries are going to have to use very different methods from ours as well as many of the same. In particular whatever their—or our—words about having or avoiding "socialism," the particular combination of governmental and private efforts will vary. In India Nehru and his associates talk constantly of developing a "socialist pattern of society." We talk of avoiding "socialism." Yet a very much larger proportion of our national income and national product is governmental than in India. On the other hand, the Indian government is building steel mills because they are basic to India's development and sufficient private investment is not available—nor do the Indians think that private control of so key a factor as steel is desirable. We don't go in for public steel production—but we do have public power (and quarrel over it politically). What Nehru means by a "socialist pattern of society" is, essentially, directing economic development in the common interest and avoiding centers of private power. We have anti-trust laws to combat private economic power, and progressive taxation, eminent domain, etc. to direct development in the public interest. And so it goes. It will be interesting to see what pattern of individual enterprise, cooperative enterprise, governmental enterprise, individual-governmental partnership or whatever emerges in Ghana.

All here send love. I wished mightily that I were accompanying Maida all the way, and not just from Vienna to Washington as she sets out on her journey.

Love, Skipper

Maida Springer had been to Africa and managed to stop over in Accra to see Pauli. Lina is keeping up her barrage of letters, apparently hoping to support Pauli's morale and to dissuade her from coming home early. Like many of her general political outlook, Lina saw hope in John F. Kennedy's election as president.

✈ November 13, 1960 [AIRLETTER]
Dear Pixie,

Maida has been here this week-end with her first hand report of you and your household. How we all wished to see it in the flesh! The only thing that had us worried was Smokey's ego what with God Bless and Congo and all the other competition for his mistress's attention and affection. I do hope you manage to restore his sense of central importance in your life.

Maida gave us a good sense of your hard work, some of the inevitable strains, the excellence of your teaching, and your satisfaction from it, and all the involvements arising from the needs of your household. This is certainly a rich and rare experience all around. She told us how successful your cocktail party was in spite of the very short notice and the fact that there were competing activities that night. Congratulations on your debut as a Ghanian hostess. Altogether her report left me feeling very good about the way your experience and life are going even though you may be a bit homesick now and again.

Rene[e] sent me the check to reimburse for the travel advance. Thanks. When I think of what a fine trip you had on the Tatia and what a horrible three weeks the lonely journey on the other ship would have been, I regard this advance as a very well directed one. It now goes to the "Pauli emergency account" to be on hand for any new eventuality which may arise.

Maida, as you noted, is certainly not well and is worried about herself. She will go back to the doctor for a check up this week. I wish that she could cut down on her responsibilities to the level where she could carry them without evoking a disabling headache which requires her to lay off and rest until she gets her balance back. If she could only reach the same level of activity by staying steadily within limits instead of going over and then laying off, the same net result could be achieved with much less wear and tear, and with better chances in the long run. But I don't know how to help her to that state, for although she knows she must try to keep on an even keel she feels driven by all the things that need to be done and so finds it too difficult to relax. We'll do our best to keep her as relieved of pressure and refreshed by the farm as possible.

Needless to say we are all relieved and exhausted by the slim democratic victory and the suspense involved. For the first time since the campaign got underway Mary has been relaxed this week and I have stopped yawning sleepily as I have been since Tuesday night. Already the feel of a new breeze begins to stir in Washington. We are on tenterhooks over the cabinet appointments. especially the secretary of state. We expect Kennedy to be very independent and not to act as if he owes anything, for the vote was so confusing, the margin so close, and support from so many sources, so that nobody can claim to have "delivered" anything. There have been far too many losses of liberal democratic congressmen to make the legislative prospect happy, but [vice president-elect] Lyndon Johnson and Mr. Sam [Speaker of the House Sam Rayburn] will certainly undertake to deliver and should be able to do so successfully. In any case it is a relief to have someone positive taking over the reins of government. Maida is sending you clippings to cover the details.

Pauline Coggs was here for a political luncheon. She is in wonderful form—more herself than I have seen her for years—she was delighted to hear of you.

Much love and special post election pat for Smokey. Skipper.

As usual when Pauli sends drafts for comment, Lina responds in detail. In this case she comments on an article called "A Question of Identity," which Pauli was inspired to write by her first encounter with Africa. Ware provides a careful analysis and many suggestions for improvement.

✈ November 26, 1960

Dear Pixie,

[. . .] we started our Thanksgiving celebration with a toast to the Pixie Accra household, drunk in lovely, pink sparkling burgundy from those beautiful hollow-stemmed champagne glasses which are even lovelier when filled with burgundy than with champagne. We ended it playing the Highlife record, noting how much like Latin American, and particularly like calypso, the music is. So, you see, you were very much here. [Quite a number of people have now read and commented on "A Question of Identity."] We all think the article important [. . .] we all think it needs a bit of sharpening to make it come off with its potential force and punch. [She reports the comments of Murray's other friends and gives specifics. This is followed by line-by-line editing.][3]

I hope this does not leave you feeling like the Charlie Brown cartoon which I have over my desk in which Lucy says "You're a fool, Charlie Brown. I don't know why I waste my time even talking to you!" at which Charlie sneezes violently and observes, "I think I'm becoming allergic to criticism!"

Ware and her friends take a great interest in possible Kennedy appointments. "Soapy" Williams is G. Mennan Williams, liberal Democratic governor of Michigan, who has just been appointed assistant secretary of state for African affairs. Chester Bowles had been ambassador to India and had—in Ware's view—done a terrific job. He was reappointed to the post by President Kennedy and held it for eight more years.

⤞ December 2, 1960

Dear Pixie, or should I say "Madam Hostess"

I was delighted to get your heavy half-century letter (I hope our birthday cable arrived on schedule) full of delight in the performance of your students and your generally good outlook. I was also glad to get the clipping of Nkrumah's remarks at the farewell luncheon to [U.S.] Ambassador Flike. I sent the clipping to the editor of the *Washington Post* with a covering note saying that in view of the statements by press and public officials re Ghana's political tendencies I thought the Post's readers would be interested in the reported speech. They probably won't use it as they printed a letter from a Ghanian to the same general effect (though not using the particular speech) a day or two after I mailed my letter. [Scribbled in the margin:] Just received a note from the Post saying "sorry" but maybe the editorial writers will take note.]

Congratulations on the performance of your students. I have no doubt that you are doing a bang-up job with them. It is a delight to see them perform. I shall be most interested to see your material. I expect that it will

3. The article, which was not published when written, eventually appeared in summarized form in Pauli's autobiography, *Song in a Weary Throat.* There is a manuscript copy of the original in the Murray Papers.

become the standard text, not only for Ghana but for the other African countries. It is fun to be first in the field, for it lets you set a pattern and it gives you a very appreciative audience. But it's hard work!

I sent "Question of Identity" off to Maida, and then immediately wished that I still had it around, first for Frank Lorrimer with whom I got into a hassle because he repeated the comment on *Proud Shoes* which, he said, he had made to you, and I tried to make him see the issue as you presented it in the article, then (again) when I got to my class in Racial and Cultural Factors in Social Work Practice. Actually I should like to make it available to my students if you would be willing to have me do so. I would label it "rough draft" and "Confidential" so they would know you are still revising it and that it is unpublished. The students have brought into class a number of cases where color and identity are all mixed up with their other problems, and the students themselves have unresolved feelings that they have to recognize and handle in order to be able to help their clients. (One student has a part Indian–part Negro client who objects to the term Negro and refers to whites as "pale faces." Another spoke in class of five foster parents among his clients all of whom express ambivalent feelings around color, and of his white client who relates to him quite comfortably over the telephone but is very constrained in dealing with him face to face. And then this student comes to me out of class to talk about his own background and his own feelings which, he said, he could not speak about in class—so I told him to read *Proud Shoes*.

Helen Lockwood, incidentally, is back in the US and will be here next week. I'll capture "Identity" for her to read.

The enclosed clipping is interesting in relation to your remarks re Negroes in the foreign service. The note on American preoccupation with man's potentialities turned up in one of my clean-up spasms. I thought you would find it apt.

Want to say I feel cheered by Soapy Williams' appointment. I think he may do for Africa what Bowles did for India, in his direct, outgoing, genuinely interested and concerned way. At least, I cannot imagine finding the situation which we encountered on the Africa desks when we visited the Department last year, in a department for which Soapy was responsible.

As of this writing, we are still holding our breath and hoping against hope that Bowles will be Sec. of State. His name stays on the list of speculations. Mary, of course, is even more anxious than the rest of us, for his appointment will mean a job for her as well as the policies we all want. By the time this reaches you we shall all know.

Your enclosure with your last letter of a letter written a week before expressing concern that I had not written disturbed me as I was not aware of having lapsed in my never-too-regular correspondence. I do know how it seems to be abroad and how long intervals seem between letters— how one looks at the mail each day and feels neglected if there is not a letter. Though I have been through this on repeated absences, and though I am one of the poorest letter writers when I am home, I never fail to expect more letters than I have reason to receive and I write fewer than I myself would want to have written were I at the foreign end. And when I'm abroad I write constantly.

So if the time between my letters seems unduly long, just put it down to the fact that days have a sameness and time gets away at home, whereas abroad each day is likely to be full and special and to abound in experience that one wants to commemorate.

As for the check which I trust that I did acknowledge, I understand perfectly your feeling about both keeping the record straight and knowing that you can always fall back on the resources of the well-filled tent. As I said, I have earmarked the money Pauli's emergency fund so you know it is there when you need it. Maida's repayments go into a "what African project shall I spend this on?" account, subject to Maida's indication of preferred causes.

Even as she grows older and more sure of herself, Murray still welcomes advice about her writing from Ware, Helen Lockwood, and the rest of their close group.

✈ [Accra]
December 2, 1960
Dear Skipper:
I received your 11/25 comments on yesterday, and how I cherish this Maestro-Second Cellist relationship, Mary's prejudices re cellos notwithstanding.

As you will see when you read the enclosed, I had already begun to have second thoughts and to revise the whole piece, second-third-fourth, etc. time round. I had the completed draft at the typists when your letter arrived. And now, I must confess that I am unable to follow some of your specifics because I did a paste pot job on my copy of the 11/14 draft and it is no longer in existence. I think I've taken care of some of the phrases etc. which troubled you, but not all. I'm sending the completed draft along as is (with a thermofax copy of your comments, if I can get one) so you will have it at hand when you read the 12/2 draft. I am still bothered by that separation of *cultural* and *biological* heritages which I have not done completely in this draft, as you will see, but since the whole piece is much further along than when I last wrote you, I can be patient enough to wait until you have had an opportunity to view the entire material.

You'll be pleased to know that Harper's magazine is interested; two of their editors have read the earlier version and think it is highly interesting; Marie Rodell and Harper and Co. are both agent and publisher, respectively, of Louis Lomax "*The Reluctant*," just out, and Marie tells me this piece supplements the book in a highly interesting fashion. She will not send me the book at this stage (doesn't want to influence my view, I suspect) but I would welcome reviews of it if you happen to spot one.

I was going to mail the enclosed to Maida, but decided it would be bait for another weekend at the farm before Christmas. Naturally, I am anxious for her personal reaction, since we have been carrying on a dialogue on Africa for many years now. I recognize that my views may be colored by my particular location, but others whose experiences in this area are broader than mine feel it is valid generally. I've stressed West Africa because there may be much more leverage in East Africa and I wasn't trying to do a hatchet job, but to face facts realistically and try to create discussion along the lines of the questions I have raised. [. . .] If all goes well I expect to have a very pleasant Christmas—since I have a three weeks vacation—doing a little trekking around Ghana and perhaps going over into Upper Volta [. . .] and see the northern country where Yaro comes from. He will go of course as guide and interpreter. [. . .]

Pauli Murray was a gifted, imaginative, and hard-working teacher. She saw potential in her ill-prepared Ghanian students, and set herself to help them learn how to think for themselves.

✢ Friday, Dec 8, 1960

Dearest Skipper:

[. . .] To find that you think the piece ["A Question of Identity"] significant enough to share with your classes is really a great compliment . . . [She goes on to say she had been hopeful about Ghana, but now realizes that] we cannot rely on genuine friendship in these parts. In saying this, I make a distinction between governments and peoples.

I enclose the Constitution of Ghana, the cases I reviewed for the students [. . .], the suggested topics for term papers in order to give them experience in original research and a trial examination question which I threw at them Monday past and for which they had no advance notice [. . .]. They did surprisingly well [. . .]. Yesterday, we spent 1 and ½ hours in post mortems, discussing every phase of the exam question. [. . .] I learned something as a teacher and they learned as students. [. . .]

I gave them a pep talk and told them that I think of them as the John Marshalls, James Madisons, Thomas Jeffersons and Thurgood Marshalls of the Constitution of Ghana; that both the reputation of this law school and the future of Constitutional Law of Ghana will depend on them— since they will be the first class to graduate and will have had a more intensive study of the Constitution than any group in Ghana to date. I have also told them that their two most important tools are the ability to think and analyze dispassionately and precisely and the use of words: that if they can use these tools, they can do a job even if they do not have other resources such as law libraries and reference materials; that if I can contribute to their better use of these I will consider my job well done. [She goes into detail about her method of grading.]

[. . .] it is common knowledge that my course is the best organized and most productive in the school. The students are beginning to spend their weekends in the library here—an excellent sign. They also ask for more class time [. . .].

They are beginning to appreciate the American approach to Constitutional Law—quite a swing over from their English orientation. [She has arranged for her whole syllabus to be sent to Lina through the American Embassy.]

On December 10, 1960, Ware sends detailed comments and three pages of suggestions for the most recent draft of "A Question of Identity." In spite of all Ware's encouragement, Murray is already thinking of coming home in 1961 rather than staying for three years as she originally intended. Ware offers all kinds of praise and encouragement before she moves on to indicate her dismay that Pauli might give up this challenging opportunity—one that she sees as important for Murray and also for her students, not to mention the U.S. government, which is so much criticized in Africa.

→ December 27, 1960
Dear Pixie,

I was absolutely entranced by your examination, and by all the evidence of the magnificent job you are doing as a teacher of law. What a contribution you are making to the future of Africa, not alone of Ghana, but of other countries which will, I am sure, use your material as they develop their training programs—at least those who start from the British rather than the French background. Congratulations, and more power to you. I do hope that you are going to find it possible to continue for some time. There is a great temptation to become involved in controversy and in events which are taking place outside the classroom. But this can only get in the way of doing the real job and making the unique contribution which your teaching can make. The performance of your students is much more eloquent a testimony to what you are trying to tell people that American stands for than anything—but anything—that you or others can say [. . .] it is far better to let it speak for itself. As I see the situation—not only where you are but in many parts of the world—it is a disservice to the USA for a technician to try to defend and explain it, for this impairs the effectiveness of his demonstrating it. I often remember one of my first Howard undergraduate students who asked me at the end of the year "Are there other white people like you? If I thought so it would change all my thinking about white people." She was asking on the basis of what I was and what I did, and only when this had got through to her could she hear anything I might have said about white people; and even then my simple "yes, of course"—coupled with her own experience of working with me—was more eloquent than any number of well reasoned and factually substantiated paragraphs.

All of which is just by way of saying that your references to March and/or July saddened me, for I know how much you want to serve the

USA, not let it down, and how much you want to contribute to African development, not leave an unfinished beginning, and how much you are your own full best self in your magnificent teaching. I know the tropics, a difficult atmosphere, and some homesickness can add up to plenty of discomfort, so I shall not be without understanding whatever your course, but I can't help seeing you as a sort of national and international investment of the highest order, and wishing that it might bring in its fullest returns . . . [She reports on plans for going abroad and encloses a clipping from the *New York Times*.]

Skipper

Ware is still hoping Pauli will stick it out in Ghana a bit longer, but she approaches the matter indirectly. Her care for Maida Springer is one more example of Lina's strong sense of responsibility for her friends. John F. Kennedy is about to be inaugurated president.

→ January 19, 1961 [AIRLETTER]

Dear Pauli:

Your last two letters—including the one mailed by Bill Hastie, have filled us with delight for they have sounded so full of satisfaction and delight in a job well done and still a-doing. It was wonderful that Hastie could come to your class and to spend a couple of days with you. It seems to me that if you had made a list of all the VIPs and friends you would most like to see you could not have devised as fine an array as you have actually had in that little international center of yours, nor could you have seen them under more favorable circumstances. Whatever the strains and discomforts this has been a *rich* year.

Your lecture notes and materials arrived at school two days ago. The student who was due for a conference found me absorbed in your material when he arrived quite late, and resentful of the fact that he had not been later, for I wanted to go right on reading. It is a superb job. I would like to see it published in some form and made available in other countries. Although it is focused on the Ghana constitution, the way of presenting material is a model and the constitutional issues discussed are present in all constitutions. I don't know what would be involved in getting it into print or reproduced in some way which make it available to others, but it should be done. When it is, you will want to do a careful proofreading of the bibliographies into which some typographical errors have crept (spelling for names, etc.)

Now inauguration day is upon us, ushered in by what the 6 o'clock newscast described as a "paralyzing" snowstorm. I agreed with the description as I was waiting on the same two-mile stretch of road where I had been for 2 hours. And I had left town at 3:00 o'clock before the evening traffic started. I hate to think how many thousands of people are out there now, stalled in traffic, while we sit snugly by the fire.

I regret to report that Maida is in the hospital with a bad ulcer that nobody knew she had until it suddenly started to bleed yesterday. She is in Freedmen's under the excellent care of Dr. Kelly Brown. The hospital is so crowded that we haven't been able to get her into a private room yet—in fact there wasn't even a ward bed last night—but we trust that a private room will be vacated soon. Fortunately her mother has been visiting her and is here to be with her. It is disheartening to have this come along when she was doing quite well with her general problem of hypertension etc. It is also a mystery how it failed to have been diagnosed as she must have had it for some time and she has been examined repeatedly, hospitalized, and treated for this and that etc. It must have been masked by other conditions. From all reports she couldn't be in better hands than Kelly Brown's. I'll keep you posted as to her progress.

Renee is due here next week and with her report on Africa and Helen Lockwood will be here also. We shall await her story eagerly. Word has just come from Yugoslavia that our visit there has been arranged. Obviously bar exams etc. prevent you from spending the inter-term period in Europe. I'm tempted to come home via Accra—but we shall see. It's a bit out of the way of the direct route! Love, Skipper

On February 8 a letter indicates that Gardiner and Lina are on their way to Europe in a snowstorm. The next letter is from Austria. Means is teaching at the Salzburg Seminar and Ware is enjoying herself. Her enthusiasm for the young Europeans gives her hope for the future. Sixteen years after Europe was in shambles, a new generation is coming to the fore. Sixteen years after the end of World War II, she is optimistic about the future of Europe. She does not mention the Cold War as an obstacle to that future.

→¦ American Studies Seminar
Schloss Leopoldskron
Salzburg, Austria
February 17, 1961
Dear Pixie,

Here we are in a most interesting setting and with a most interesting group of 60 young European professionals from industry, labor, government, economic life and communications—a lively minded, serious, limber and warm hearted group. Gardiner is doing all the formal work—i.e. all the lecturing, but we all—i.e. faculty wives carry on private seminars of our own every lunch and supper with whomever we may be sitting near. We try to pick a different set of neighbors for each meal, and the talk is very varied. The subject of this month's seminar is American industry and Labor. We have a business man, a labor man and three economists, one a specialist in U.S. investment abroad (he's about to return to the states as deputy asst. sec. of commerce for international affairs). Interestingly enough, we older folks were all part of the New Deal and the defense effort at the beginning of the War and now our young colleague steps into the new generation's administration.

It is very interesting to me to be with this group of Europeans and to observe their general affluence, relaxed attitude, flexibility and pragmatism. There are a few feelings near the surface—but very few. They are neither edgy nor doctrinaire. They are interested in steps in which they are engaged—to take advantage of the European common market, to improve labor relations, to develop south Italy, etc.etc. They are interested in the U.S. and kindly disposed toward it, though ready to be jittery—a little—about U.S. investments in their countries which they both want and fear. If they are Europe's future leaders—as some are already well on the way toward being in their respective fields—it augurs well (unless they go stodgy along the route!).

The seminar is held in an 18th century "castle" built by a very worldly archbishop and renovated in the 20th century by the theatrical producer Max Reinhart. It is thoroughly authentic, except, fortunately, for the addition of modern plumbing and quite good central heat (if you don't count some of the drafty halls and stair wells). The location is beautiful, in a valley dominated by spectacular mountains on the edge of one of the most charming old towns of Europe all full of 13th–18th century churches, alleys, passages, old houses etc.etc. In the summer it is a great tourist center because the Mozart Festival is held here. But now in off-season it is pleasant and uncrowded—and all one has to do to hear Mozart is to attend High Mass in the cathedral on Sunday.

After three more weeks we shall take off for Yugoslavia—which should be interesting and good fun, too. Love, Skipper

After Yugoslavia Ware goes to Paris to work with her collaborators on the History of Mankind *volume. Murray flies to Paris to meet her, and goes with her and Gardiner to visit Lina's collaborator in Holland. She and Ware also go to England. This is Murray's first trip to Europe, and everything is new and exciting. She can hardly believe she is actually meeting so many famous people and seeing the sights of which she has so long read.*

Ware's last days in Paris turn exciting in an unexpected way after a coup in Algeria.

By late April, Ware is headed home. She refers to a problem, presumably about her appointment at Howard, and makes an uncharacteristic comment about continuing as Mrs. Gardiner Means rather than as Dr. Caroline Farrar Ware. She may have been momentarily tempted, but her pattern had been set and would continue for the rest of her life.

⤴ Over the Atlantic
April 26, 1961
Dear Pixie,

I hope your Pan Am flight was as pleasant as this one and the rest of your trip to Accra went well.

I must say that I fell into this plane with a big sigh of delight, for after days of battle I was ready to leave Paris. I was tempted to join my brother and sister-in-law and drive with them back to Holland to see the tulips— and if the political situation in Paris had got worse I might have done so. But my sight seeing days are over for the nonce, and as soon as I got a memorandum of understanding signed by my chairman this morning I scrambled for a cab, missed the bus to Orly that I was aiming for, as we did yours, but took the next in plenty of time—writing my last memos in the bus to mail at Orly. In these days I think that I covered all angles and did the best I could have done with the situation. Here's hoping things come out okay.

The sudden Algiers coup, and its equally sudden collapse, caught Paris completely by surprise and gave us four days of suspense when no one knew whether paratroops would start dropping, whether the tanks that rumbled into place around the Chambre des Deputés would be called into action and whether the thousands of civilians who responded to the call to "come into the streets" would have to man the barricades. Planes were grounded at Sunday midnight and resumed at midday. Pan Am on Tuesday recommended its 1:30 rather than the 9 o'clock flight today as less likely to be delayed. I could not check my bag at Les Invalides as I wanted to or at least I was told yesterday that I would not be able to because bombs went off on Sunday in the baggage room of three stations so all the baggage departments were closed. Last night's headlines read or rather screamed "Debé says blood may flow tomorrow." This morning's headline said "Algeria coup es [illegible]." So there we are. Those "algérie française" signs were against DeGaulle's Algeria policy. But when the generals went off the reservation De Gaulle's strength apparently held though the news blackout was almost complete and nobody knew what was going on. The "manifestation" that we saw last week was reflected in a different form—workers walked out, public transportation stopped, etc. from 5 hrs to 6 hrs on Monday a manifestation to support DeGaulle! Now hope to see what is stuck and what wasn't there and to find my next assignment. Must say that I have so enjoyed the role of Mrs. G.C. Means that I am tempted to remain in it. The last days of struggle as Dr. C.F.W. haven't made me ache to resume my professional personality. Will call Maida tomorrow and give her a report on Pixie the traveler. [...] Love Skipper

Murray decides to come home in 1961 and somehow has managed to wangle a fellowship—again from the Ford Foundation—to support a year or two at Yale, where she plans to take a doctorate in law. By this time, Ware is resigned to her return.

→ June 4, 1961

Dear Pixie,

My copy of your letter to the Atty General with the "lesson" attached came to port yesterday. The lesson is brilliant—and you do lay it on the line with the "provocative question."

Have you sent the Atty General letter to the N.Y.Times or the Washington Post? Mary, Maida and I think it should see publication. If you haven't sent it we suggest you do—preferably, Mary and I think, to the Post. (I didn't ask Maida which.)

Did Harold Isaacs read your piece "What is Africa to Me?" He has written almost the identical article—very well—for the May 13 issue of the New Yorker, with all your points, and a few more (e.g. American girls married to Africans) I'll save it for you in case the N.Yorker doesn't get to Accra.

Maida's squeal of delight when I told her of your Yale fellowship almost ripped out the telephone line. We're counting the days. Love, Skipper

By the time the next letter is written on November 17, 1961, Murray is back in the United States to take up the fellowship to do advanced work in law at Yale Law School. Ware, meantime, has been appointed to a UN mission to Ceylon, where she will go in the spring. Both are hoping William Hastie will be appointed to the Supreme Court.

In July 1962, Murray sends a long report on her Ghana sojourn to a list of friends, apologizing for the scarcity of letters during her time there. She describes her new situation in New Haven in humorous detail and then goes on to say that her eighteen months in Ghana had been exciting, astringent, challenging, and rewarding.

The report is candid to a point, well written and informative about the complexities of African politics and the challenges facing newly independent states. She provides colorful detail about things she had witnessed, people she had met, trips she had taken. No one, reading this report, would guess that she had spent the many miserable hours reported on in her journal.

She winds up with a plea for money to help two African students who have opportunities to study in the United States if they can manage

airfare. In a typical gesture, she has advanced them the money with faith that her friends will come through, which they do.

When Ware returns from Ceylon, she and Means begin writing letters in an effort to find a publisher willing to bring out a paperback edition of Proud Shoes.

In August of 1963, Murray, who had recently visited Yellow Head Island, takes part in the March on Washington. She also goes to Freedmen's Hospital, where her sister Mildred works, for a checkup.

➤ 96 York Square
New Haven, Conn
September 5, 1963
Dear Skipper:
[. . .] By now Mary has told you the exciting details of the March, August 28. It was a great day—and Bonnie and I did march for you and Gardiner. Having marched up to the Memorial, we reversed ourselves and marched all the way back to the Washington Monument to see the depth of the crowd. It was indescribable.

[She then goes into detail about her health, and says that the work-up revealed that she did not have heart trouble, but rather a small hiatal hernia.]

Meanwhile, the USIA [United States Information Agency] was so impressed with the Radcliffe piece[4] I have received a written offer to prepare a thirty to forty thousand word manuscript on "race relations" for distribution in the French speaking African areas [. . .]. They offer $1250 for a completed manuscript and all French language rights and possibly Latin-American rights [. . .].

[She plans to defer the Ford Foundation fellowship meant for her to use at Yale for a year, while she writes the USIA book and possibly another book for Harper. She asks if it would be convenient for Ware to lend her what she needs until she is paid for the USIA job at the time the book is finished.]

4. Pauli Murray, "The Law as It Affects Desegregation," *Radcliffe Quarterly* 47, no. 3 (August 1963): 19–28. The article was entered into the record during the congressional hearings on the Civil Rights Bill of 1964.

In 1961 President Kennedy appointed a Commission on the Status of Women, with Eleanor Roosevelt as its Chairman. Caroline Ware was a member of the commission, which had only one African American member, Dorothy Height, president of the National Council of Negro Women. Much of its work was carried out by committees made up of people with special knowledge of the subject under consideration. Pauli Murray, on the initiative of an old friend, and doubtless with Ware's support, was appointed to the Committee on Civil and Political Rights, where she exerted considerable influence.

She was also very active in support of Title VII of the Civil Rights Act of 1964, the section that added sex to the list of bases on which a person's rights could not be infringed under protection of the federal government. Many members of Congress were scornful of that provision and wanted to remove it from the final bill.

Murray worked with Dorothy Height, Marguerite Rawalt, and other representatives of nongovernmental agencies to support the women in Congress who wanted to protect Title VII by preventing hostile amendments to the bill. She supplied them with data, as she did for a few male supporters, such as Minnesota senator Hubert Humphrey.

Murray also did important work for the Commission on the Status of Women. The commission's final report noted:

The opinion of members of the Committee and the Commission were strongly influenced by a document prepared at the request of the Committee by [. . .] Miss Pauli Murray [. . .]. She concluded that the Supreme Court, if presented with an appropriate test case, would today interpret the Fourteenth Amendment as prohibiting unreasonable discrimination based on sex [. . .].[5]

Murray had sought to put an end to the long conflict about the Equal Rights Amendment with this argument. She would make the same case in an article written with Mary Eastwood in the George Washington University Law Review in December 1965 called "Jane Crow and the Law: Sex Discrimination and Title VII," in which she and Eastwood

5. Margaret Mead and Frances Balgley Kaplan, eds., American Women: The Report of the President's Commission on the Status of Women and Other Publications of the Commission (New York: Charles Scribner's Sons, 1965), 149–51.

equated the evil of antifeminism with that of racism. Since Murray had had a good deal to do with the passage of Title VII, she was anxious not to see it defanged. As one of the earliest authoritative works dealing with the legal implications of feminism, the article was often cited by crusading feminists.

In 1966, Ware and Murray were both present when a group impatient with the progress of women under the law joined to set up the National Organization for Women, popularly known as NOW. After serving briefly on the board of the organization, in 1967 Murray resigned because she felt the concerns of middle-class white women were taking precedence over the needs of poor women, especially black women. She also supported her Fourteenth Amendment argument, while other members of the NOW board were resolute in promoting the Equal Rights Amendment. She remained on good terms with some members of the board, but the needs of black people were her central concern. In her autobiography she talks about her part in founding NOW but says nothing about her break with the board.

She continued to be much involved with work for women's rights. She joined the board of the American Civil Liberties Union and, working with future Supreme Court justice Ruth Bader Ginsburg, became one of its strong advocates for women, black and white. She helped write the brief for the case of White v. Crook, which challenged the constitutionality of all-male, all-white juries in Lowndes County, Alabama. After a unanimous decision in favor of the plaintiffs by the U.S. District Court, the attorney general of Alabama decided not to appeal, so the change became law for the area covered by the three-judge court from the Middle District of Alabama. Of wider significance, it became an example to other states where women and black people were excluded from jury service.

In 2005 Justice Ginsburg wrote:

Pauli was among a small band of women on the ACLU's National Board determined to propel the Union into becoming a lead player in the effort to secure equal citizenship stature for women. When I co-authored the brief for appellant Sally Reed in the turning point gender discrimination case, Reed v. Reed, 404 U.S. 71 (1971) I placed Pauli's name on the cover together with Dorothy Kenyon's. Both *women had urged, a decade and more earlier, arguments that courts were not prepared to hear until the 1970s [. . .] descriptive words for a portrait of Pauli:—independent, intelligent, poetic, feisty, determined, confident in her counsel to the Union. I was drawn to her for her courage and conviction [. . .].*[6]

6. Personal communication, March 2005, in response to my query asking her to characterize Murray from her experience on the ACLU Board.

➤ 5

WRITING,

EDITING, AND

BRANDEIS

By 1965 Murray had completed her course work at Yale and was writing a dissertation titled "Roots of the Racial Crisis: A Prologue to Policy." Harper and Row, which had published *Proud Shoes*, expressed an interest in publishing the volume if she could turn it into a readable book. Working very hard to that end, she relies as heavily as ever on Ware's editorial skill. Her confidence in her mentor is justified: Ware responds to the draft. She provides the kind of editorial help a writer dreams of. The advice she offers has broader applications beyond the work at hand.

➤ July 11, 1965

Dear Pixie:

On a fine rainy and foggy island day, I read The Great Work from cover to cover (minus the footnotes). It is a fine, solid, persuasive job. Let us hope that it finds a publisher soon. [. . .]

From the point of view of publication, I have a few general comments. I was bothered at first by your constant "as so-and-so says." Much of the time, of course, you want to quote directly and attribute in the text, not just in the notes. I should be a little happier if you went through the text and knocked out the *unnecessary* "so-and-so says" and especially "in the words of" [line editing of the revised manuscript follows. Knowing as I do, with the benefit of hindsight, that the manuscript will not, in the end, be published because the readers for publishers think there is not much original in it, I believe that in the next paragraph Ware, a careful historian herself, is trying gently to suggest that perhaps Murray is out of her depth.]

In order to catch any lapses in scholarship, such as the items noted on p. 17 of Chapter I, I think it would be good to have the respective chapters or sections read by appropriate specialists who can catch small points of your failing to be at home in the latest material in the way a specialist is—an impossibility, of course, in a work that ranges as this does.

The Island misses you, and will welcome you with open arms when you come. Percy is the same old sixpence and asks after you and Renee. Gardiner has great projects. I am still awaiting my page proofs. [. . .] Love, Skipper

Pauli took Lina's comments seriously.

→ July 20, 1965
Dear Skipper:
I know you and Gardiner share the sense of loss with Adlai [Stevenson]'s going. As you said of Mrs. R., it leaves a big hole. I know of no eloquent voice which can fill the void. [There follows a paragraph about having her teeth replaced and one about getting trifocals.] Was glad to get your comment on the dissertation. "A fine, solid persuasive job" is like receiving another degree "in absentia." I was working on the Introduction when your letter arrived. Have incorporated your suggestions in the Intro, cut out much of the law, science and policy jargon, sharpened the personal experience of teaching in Africa and incorporated some of the President's June 4 speech in it. Hope to send you draft copy soon, because I think the Introduction is crucial to the success of the work. Also hope to have C. Vann Woodward read for historical accuracy, and perhaps a psychologist for other materials. Harper and Row report one "enthusiastic" reading, and ms. now being read by second reader. [. . .] Love to both of you

As Murray works on the revision of her dissertation, she continues to rely on Ware for editorial help.

→ July 23, 1965
Dear Skipper:
I'm enclosing draft of the revised Introduction which I think has met some of your questions as well as my own and Tom Emerson's[1] com-

1. Thomas Emerson was a noted civil rights attorney on the faculty of the Yale University Law School.

ments. I've tried to make the whole approach more up to date, to include the African experience so as to sharpen the focus and indicate the impelling reason for such a work, and have indicated content to inform the reader what to expect. The McDougal material has come out and will go in footnote or appendix. [. . .]

Feel a great burden removed in getting this Introduction in shape. Feel that it will set the tone of the whole work and make the rest of the revision comparatively simple, perhaps occasional rearrangement will take care of most of the suggestions plus anticipatory statements and better opening paragraphs.

Ware replies. As always, she tries to tether Murray to the real world, urging her to replace abstractions and sweeping claims with concrete stories and realistic generalizations.

↘ July 27, 1965
Dear Pixie,

I plucked your mss. out of the P.O. en route to Machias, read it in the bus from Machias to Bangor, am now on the Boston-Bangor plane and will mail it back to you from Boston. Service?!

I like what you have done with the introduction. My editorial comments are minor as you see. I hope you can read them in spite of this bumpy bus. My general comments are even fewer. I don't like your use of "one" and "it is believed." I would prefer "the author" or "I". What you say is fine. It is just a matter of construction. When talking about Africa you say, anonymously, "he points out" or "asserts" "tries" etc. You are describing your own reactions. I changed these verbs to "may point out" and "may assert" for you cannot treat this as a universal reaction. The alternative would be to treat it frankly as personal. You found yourself in this position and reacted in this manner. On the next page you ask your reader to "conjure up" and "try to imagine" the faces of your students and their skepticism. Much better to say that you faced these faces or attitudes. Again at the end I would use "the author" and "I." Your statement about involvement and objectivity is good. My editorial suggestions are designed to understate the point rather than overstate it, and thus, I think, make it stronger.

The editorial suggestions on pages 11 and 16 are designed to keep you from sounding utopian or doctrinaire by talking about "a choice by the American people" or "a reorganization of American society." As you well know, history rarely moves by "a choice" and certainly "the American people" are not going to "choose" in one dramatic moment to resolve "the problem" once and for all. It is a matter of many choices, pointed in a common direction. And unless you mean to associate your recommendations with a revolutionary take-over of the October Revolution type, you don't want to link them to "a reorganization" but rather to a host of cumulating, crucial changes.

On the point about the derivation of the term "slavery" I would drop the sentence and say nothing about the controversy. The derivation of the word is of no consequence for your purposes. I caught the sentence as I read because it seemed to recall the Latin and Greek words "esclavos" or some thing like that and I made a note to tell you to look up the Latin when the anthropologist arrived and started talking about the Hammurabi code on which he is working, which includes monetary and other compensations for injuries, done by and to "freemen" (apparently the superior class), the equivalent of peasants and slaves, it occurred to me to ask him the Latin and Greek words for slave. He wondered why I asked— so I showed him the passage.

On the matter of conquest as a source, I would simply, on the page following the definition in where you sum up (don't have the text before me for accurate reference) change "most" slavery as result of conquest to "much" or say "most African slavery"—this takes care of everything.

Glad the editing is going well [. . .].

Even with Ware's help, Pauli does not manage to create a book on which a publisher is willing to take a chance. The study survives in the Yale University library.

As she approaches graduation with her J.D.S. in view, Murray applies for an opening on the faculty of the Yale Law School. When she is turned down, she is mortified by having to stay on to finish. She reflects that few women are teaching in law schools, and certainly not in the ones to which she aspires.

When she turned to law firms, the situation was not much better. Even the Yale degree and her fine dissertation are not enough to overcome

their general reluctance to hire women. A black woman in her 60s probably did not seem a very good bet to most old-line firms, and she wanted
only the best. She never speaks of a possible return to Paul, Weiss. She
supports herself for a while by again writing material for the Methodist
women, and in the fall of 1966 she serves briefly as a consultant to
the Equal Employment Opportunity Commission established under the
Civil Rights Act of 1964. She had criticized the EEOC for ignoring the
provision of the bill that made sex a prohibited ground for discrimination, and pointed out that only one or possibly two of the commissioners
had any sympathy for Title VII of the law. Now, looking for a niche, she is
a candidate for a permanent job with the commission. Notes in her
journal characterize her interview for the job as a "grilling," which she
finds offensive; she also indicates there that she feels herself an appropriate person to be on the Commission itself rather than to be employed by
it. This whole episode is yet another major disappointment. There is
some evidence that her earlier association with the Lovestone Communists had come back to haunt her since candidates for commission jobs
were undoubtedly screened for loyalty.

Disappointed or not, she has to eat, and when she is offered the vice
presidency of Benedict College, a woman's college in South Carolina, she
takes it and describes it to her friends as a great opportunity.

From almost the first day, things do not go well at Benedict. She
arrives on campus even before her official appointment begins, and immediately starts trying to reorganize the place. The president, who had
appointed her, tries in vain to persuade her to stay within her official
responsibilities, but she continues to do things her way. She has some
success in raising grant money, and has what appear to be some good
ideas, but she manages to alienate most of the administrators. At the
end of one year she leaves in a rage, initially blaming everybody but
herself. On later reflection, however, the experience leads to some serious
introspection.

In April of 1967 her journal entry is still bemoaning the failure of her
hope to be appointed a commissioner at EEOC. In November she reflects
on her break with NOW (a subject on which the letters have nothing to
say) and on the fact that she could not shape the organization to her own
views. Writing notes on her resignation, she characterizes those who had
opposed her views as "ferocious" and adds, "I saw a leadership that was

so venomous it was painful to try to speak. The only wise thing to do was to withdraw and consolidate my personal resources."

Nevertheless this affair too seems to lead to introspection. After all these events, on December 4, 1967 she makes a list in her journal of what she takes to be her weaknesses.

- *undue sensitivity*
- *fierce outbursts of resentful anger*
- *acquisitive in an egotistic way*
- *lack of cooperation with associates*
- *intuitive rather than professional*
- *redoubtable opponent*
- *administrative talents not outstanding*
- *selfishness*
- *deceit*
- *vanity*
- *much self-approbation*
- *vindictive*
- *bullying*
- *unscrupulous disposition*
- *cunning methods in gaining goals*
- *slow to admit error*

[. . .]

- *fault-finding*
- *ill-nature*
- *tendency toward copying and plagiarism*

In June of 1968 while she is trying to figure out what to do next, Murray is invited to visit Brandeis University with the possibility of an appointment to the faculty. While she is considering how she might respond, an invitation to participate in a meeting of the World Council of Churches to be held in Uppsala, Sweden, arrives. Both these opportunities elicit an enthusiastic letter from Ware.

→ July 10, 1968
Dear Pixie,
Delighted to find your letter when I got back from Venezuela Sunday. I managed to read my mail before taking to the telephone and thus learned that you had got away earlier in the week. What a fine junket. A bit

of Northern Europe is just what the doctor ordered—though I must say my personal recollection of Uppsala is a bit dim. Gardiner and I bicycled there in 1939 and they wouldn't believe that the obvious tramp was really a distinguished American scholar. The heel-clicking, collar-tie-and-jacket professorial style was very much in evidence.

As for Brandeis, I have all fingers crossed and breath held for it is just exactly right. If it does come through I feel sure that your troubles and wandering will be over. I have long insisted that you belong in a teaching situation. Brandeis has the general orientation, flexibility, imagination etc. that make it a suitable setting for you; the assignment is challenging and really down the middle of your alley; the fact that you are being brought by a new president whom you know and who knows you favors your stature and the opportunity to make the most of the situation. Even though the Boston area isn't New York, it has many positive features that you will enjoy. And you are halfway to Yellow Head Island. What more?

When Brandeis offers Murray a job, she decides to take it, while dreaming of being invited back to Yale. The Brandeis experience turns out to be rocky. The surviving letters do not reveal very much about the developing scene; most of what can be learned of her point of view comes from her journal notes. Apparently Ware wrote her on October 29, 1968, and on November 2 she responded, but the letters are missing.

⤳ 8B Maple Avenue (rear)
Cambridge Mass. 02139
11/2/68
Dear Skipper:
[She asks for information about NOW. Presumably Ware, who was still a member of the executive committee, knew of her angry resignation, so possibly this is a veiled effort to find out how her departure is viewed by the members. She also asks for information about someone named Jean Cahn, who had analyzed "extra legal grievances," presumably of women.]

[. . .] I have been doing some thinking on extra legal grievances, myself, as you will see from the enclosed memo to Adam Yarmolinsky. This came about because I used my Faculty admission card to the Harvard Law School forum for the first time on October 25. The topic was

"Organizing the Ghetto"; the participants were: Yarmolinsky, Moderator; Joseph Alsop; Saul Alinsky, and Thomas I. Atkins, only Negro Boston City Councilman and a student at Harvard Law. I threw the question at the panel from the floor, after commenting that the panel was wholly un-representative—that half of the population was absent, namely women. This got a big hand and laugh from the audience, a goodly number of whom were women.

Humor aside, please read the Memo and let me have your comments. [. . .]

Murray arrives at Brandeis full of ideas for developing courses that will combine her legal training with her knowledge of history. She sees bringing legal training into an undergraduate curriculum as a significant innovation, which it certainly is. Her former students recall that she demanded the best from them and in so doing raised the level of what they expected of themselves.

What she had not counted on was the appearance on campus of a group of militant young black students who come to her class prepared to do battle. Some of them are pre-freshmen—students who have to make up requirements before they qualify for admission to Brandeis and who are in no way prepared for the kind of teaching she does so well. She has to adjust her plans for the class accordingly. She reports that colleagues tell her that the course is getting high praise from some of the other students, but the advocates of black power give her a hard time. She is, they say, insufficiently "black." When they take over the administration building (which includes her office), she has difficulty finding ground on which to stand. She does not agree with what she understands the students to mean by black power, and calls herself an "integrationist-moderate." Yet she doesn't identify with the administration either.

As is her wont, she is soon engaged in confrontations with those in authority. She is profoundly offended that, as the only lawyer on the faculty, she is not asked to be part of the group trying to develop a response to the student takeover. She tells herself that Brandeis president Morris Abram has adopted her own position ("stand firm") and wants all the credit and therefore wishes to keep her out of the picture. She goes through a great deal of private soul searching as to why she is so unsympathetic to the student protestors.

She comes to believe that she had been hired as "window dressing" to placate the black students and that the faculty does not take her seriously or respect her accomplishments.

Living in Cambridge, Murray casts an eye on Harvard as a place she would like to teach. That this aspiration was not precisely a secret may be inferred from the fact that Mary Norris gave her a Harvard banner as a Thanksgiving gift.

The surviving Ware-Murray letters do not reveal much about the Brandeis experience, though judging by a letter in which Lina urges Pauli to concentrate on teaching and the woman question while staying out of the political battle, they must have discussed the situation. Ware and Means make two trips to Boston to see Murray and offer what help they can for her rebellious state of mind. The surviving letters deal with other matters, especially with the autobiography that Murray is striving to write.

Her long-established habit of sending drafts to Ware for comment continues; the following letter is in response to an early draft of some part of the autobiography. Pauli recognizes Lina's insights as valid.

→ August 15, 1971

Dear Pixie: I read the "Bundle from Boston" with great interest and puzzlement, interest for obvious reasons, puzzlement because I didn't really know what to say. So I got out *Proud Shoes* and read it to Dorothy Jackson (who had read bits when it was in process but was away when it came out) and I was reminded how terribly good that book is, what a world, or series of worlds and personalities, it brings to life, how pithy its quotes and telling its phrases and what an image emerges of the little girl, reacting to all this, shaping her identity and seeking ways to establish her sense of belonging.

And that told me part of why I was puzzled in my reaction to the new mss. If it was written for the person who has read Proud Shoes (and it does seem as if it should be a sequel) much has already been said. There is new material in this manuscript about your parents and siblings but we already know Aunt Pauline well. If it were building directly on Proud Shoes, there would be differences in selection and emphasis—a recapitulation and some complementary material, rather than a presentation de novo. On the other hand, if it is addressed to a reader who does not know

Proud Shoes, then the question is "Does it do what Proud Shoes does, plus the complementary addition?" and the answer to that is "no." The quality of life and people that you managed to convey so superbly in Proud Shoes (and remember how you struggled through many drafts to achieve this) does not come through.

Going back to Proud Shoes made me ask myself what I expect of your autobiography. And I realized again how very difficult it is to give any autobiography the right pitch. I'm aware of the problem in general because several people have tried to persuade me to write my own and I have toyed with the idea, only to be utterly baffled by the question of approach. I know you have given your approach lots of thought—you were trying to get some first paragraphs right when you were at the Island three or four years ago. At that time I didn't try to help think the problem through beyond listening to bits of specific phraseology. But now I have to, if I'm going to say anything useful about the present manuscript and your future chapters.

What do I expect of your autobiography? I expect something very different from *Proud Shoes*. That book is so distinctive and special in its quality that a *similar* book about yourself would be anti-climactic, or would invite unnecessary comparison. Yet in a fundamental way *it has to be* a similar book because it is the story, in a different generation, of the person struggling to overcome, to be and to belong.

So how achieve a different quality in your personal narrative? I think you have to give the manuscript a title. You know about Agatha Christie don't you? When asked how she gets her plots she says "From the title. Once I have the title the book writes itself." The right title says what you want the book to say. You knew from the start that "Proud Shoes" was what that book was saying, whoever or whatever the immediate subject of each chapter would be.

I can think of a number of things your new book might say, all of them projections of the drives which have carried you from cause to cause and from one level of personal achievement and development to another, in reciprocal interrelation. You would have to pick the one that speaks for you.

I think you might have a hang-up on one crucial point of emphasis or orientation. You have had a long series of external struggles. A narrative account of these, with the ramifications of personal contacts (e.g. Eleanor

Roosevelt) and in relation to the changing scene would make a fascinating book. At the same time you had an internal struggle for identity and belonging, colored by the characteristics of your antecedents and circumstances and by the ups and downs of your physico-psycho equilibrium. The chapters you have just written lay the ground work for this second struggle. If the focus of the book is to be mainly psychological—how a Negro woman with your background, generation and circumstance puts and keeps the pieces of herself together [. . .]—you might handle it one way, and I would have one set of comments on the present material. If it is to be mainly socio-political, a reflection of the changing scene in the life of a Negro woman activist and pioneer (with of course special personal qualities not to be overlooked or underrated) the line would be different, and the present material would serve differently. At the moment I lean toward this second alternative.

Well, this isn't much help. I'm delighted that you have got something down. I would not suggest trying to rework it until you have done much more and can see what it needs to serve the ultimate purpose of the book.

All power to you!

Love, Skipper

Murray finds the autobiography hard going. Some readers have commented that Song in a Weary Throat *is not as well done as* Proud Shoes. *The letter that follows suggests some of the reasons that might be the case. It also shows where Murray's mind is in the late summer of 1971.*

→ August 19, 1971

Dear Skipper:

As a follow up to my air-card acknowledging return of Mss. let me respond to your letter of 8/15. I've watched you and Gardiner spend a whole day and part of a night discussing one or another of your creative efforts and wish that dialogue were possible, but it will help me to clarify my thoughts to dash this off to you.

I was astounded anew by the depth of your insights and/or my capacity to communicate my confusion and ambivalence through the written word. You tracked my mind beautifully—title, approach, relationship to *Proud Shoes,* whose story is this? a continuation of the family or *my very own,* but since the family had such an impact in shaping my early years how to communicate that impact to a reader who does not know P.S. without intruding upon the earlier book; whether ultimately to rewrite P.S. and my own story as part of one book, in two parts, etc. etc.—all of this you get in the current ms.

Also, the significant thing which came through to me was a very real question as to whether an active individual should attempt an auto-biography for publication or merely leave a record to supply insights to future biographers. I wondered whether I should not do a book which stops around the time I finished college—and let the record speak for itself. Or to bring the book up to the point where I began to glimpse a vision of the *human* race rather than the "white and colored" races. I also have problems of my interaction with my siblings and whether the struggle to overcome the "curse" should be told in their lifetimes. In Proud Shoes I was an observer—in the sequel, I am a participant—immediately the approach becomes different.

The confusion is also reflected in my ability, or rather lack of ability, to select a title which gives focus: I've toyed with the following "Inch by Inch," "The First Wave" (my parents were the first wave of free Negroes after Emancipation,) but my story is essentially The Second Generation, "Double Jeopardy" or "Double Jeopardy—Race and Sex" (just thought this one up) "Diary, (Reflections) of an "Integrationist" etc. etc.

[She goes on to say that she tried to get down "total recall" and to keep going until she got beyond family influence into college, etc. She is clearly using Ware as a sounding board as she struggles with the numerous issues presented by the effort to write this book. She looks back to *Proud Shoes*.]

The strength of Proud Shoes, I think, was the capacity of the writer to involve the reader in the personalities and to bring the personalities alive. But there was a burning necessity to write that book—the McCarthy era had challenged my "past associations" and I wanted to tell who were my "past associations." The author was almost 20 years younger, still not established, still almost the "hungry artist in the garret," and with tremendous nervous energy. The present author is not "fat" by any means, but more mellow and less financially insecure but established in several areas and thus subject to demands which were not made during the writing of P.S. All this makes a difference in the emotional tone of the book. Yet the desire is to make the reader laugh and cry simultaneously, and there is a very real question whether this can be accomplished within the context of writing law review articles, making speeches, meeting the challenges of Brandeis U. students and Boston U. Law students and having only a few weeks each summer to get back into the practice of creative writing. [She tells of a letter from Marchette Chute[2] describing the way one author, after laboring for years on a book, realized it wasn't working, threw away the manuscript, and wrote a completely different book.]

Fortunately, Skipper, I do not have to think consciously of the ms. during the immediate future but plan to consign it to the unconscious and pull it out and reflect upon while driving, etc. I think it may fall into place either as "Notes for My Biographer" which may never be published while I am alive or that the whole first part of the book as written in ms. be discarded as "Notes" and the story pick up as a woman—friendship with Mrs. R., struggle against the U. of N.C. etc. etc. following your second alternative of a book that is "mainly socio-political, as a reflection of the changing scene in the life of a Negro woman activist and pioneer (with of course special personal qualities not to be overlooked or underrated). This also tends to strike my fancy, because I'm beginning to want to say things about "the second stage of creative non-violence," the recognition of psychic as well as physical violence and the need to transform psychic violence into creative activity, the use of physical and psychical non-violence one-to-one as well as group relationships and the self revolution which precedes the use of creative non-violence in social change. Mary Daly[3] calls this "the power of presence."

This might be a separate chapter/book, or it might come out as a reflection in autobiographical terms. It is forecast in many of my public speeches, and it is about time I begin to systematize my thinking about it. Almost everything I do which I call sometimes "pixie-like" or "magic" is part of an experimentation in imaginative "creative non-violence" which, I am more and more convinced, does work on many situations [. . .].

2. Marchette Chute (1909–94) was a prolific writer. She published poetry, history, and fiction.

3. Mary Daly is a controversial feminist philosopher who was teaching at this time at Boston College. She has challenged the church fathers over and over, and has become something of a feminist icon. She and Pauli were friends.

Lina continues to think about the autobiography she has so long urged Pauli to write. Most likely, she also hopes that her earlier letter has not stopped Pauli in her tracks, as criticism—even positive criticism— sometimes did.

⤞ [Yellow Head Island]
September 20, 1971
Dear Pixie, The Whole hog (no mere bacon)
The mail which took my card saying Please write re health brought letter with the *two pieces* of magnificent news—Professor and healthy— great, great on all counts.

I know what book you should write—just a straight, unvarnished narration of your life activities entitled Up the *Hard* Way. Its opening gambit could be either: "Operation Bootstraps" is much too advanced a concept for this climb, for it presumes both boots, and straps to lift by— and I started with neither. Or: Hitch your wagon to the furthest visible star but never stop pulling it up the rocky, rutty road, even when it seems to be headed over a cliff or turning into an untraversable path.

I got to thinking about that fragmented curriculum vitae of yours and about the kids who think that there's some easy way to have it made and whose imaginations do not encompass the process of struggle, only that of protest. And I thought the straight, hard story would have a kind of direct meaning that a more introspective one or a more searching one wouldn't have for the young. It could be done easily, without the kind of sweat that the books we corresponded about earlier would require, or that has gone into *Proud Shoes* and those four chapters this summer that came along later.

Just an idea—your letter made me sorrier than ever that my Saturday call didn't go through so that I could congratulate you. I'll try Wednesday evening when I shall be on shore for a speech to the local college—Love, Skipper
P.s. I showed your letter to [Maine senator Edmund] Muskie and Mike's [Michael Murray, Pauli's nephew] memo to incoming Science H.S. fresh- men, to the editor of the local paper and his wife, secretary of the local Democratic Party, whose parents are old friends of Ed Muskie—they were impressed by both—like me—S

When Morris Abram resigned from Brandeis and a new president took over, Murray had expected to have an easier time getting along with the administration. However, the new president decided to delay considering her for tenure. According to her journal, she was determined to resign in protest against this delay. She wrote in notes to herself that she had enjoyed nothing about Brandeis except her teaching. Yet Joyce Antler argues that she made a significant contribution to the improvement of women's situation at the University.[4] It is hard to unravel all the complications. The pages in her journal following the record of her decision to resign have been torn out. Somehow, by 1971 she is able to announce to her friends and mentors that she will soon have a chaired professorship. I have not discovered how this was brought about.

At the same time she is backing into the idea of nominating herself for the Supreme Court, and speaks of responding to Divine Guidance in making the proposal. This episode suggests something about Murray's view of her own capacities (which she sees as limited only by the circumstances of her life), and her sky-is-the-limit ambition. I have not found a response to her plan from the Ware-Means household. The New York Times *ran a brief article when she told a reporter of her desire to be considered for the Supreme Court, but, except for that, her bold venture seems to have attracted little attention.*

→| September 22, 1971

To: Hons. Captain Skipper

RE: Pixies on the Supreme Court

[The letter opens with a report on her health, which, it appears, is better than she had expected.]

Political Activities:—The tremendous emotional release of not thinking one might drop dead any minute had some rather odd results. Mike Murray and I, driving away from Mass. General Hospital, rolled along in high glee trying to out top one another in gleeful jokes. Radio in car announced retirement of Mr. Justice Black, and we opined that a master stroke on the part of President Nixon would be to appoint a woman to

---

4. Joyce Antler, "Pauli Murray: The Brandeis Years," *Journal of Women's History* 14, no. 2 (Summer 2002): 78–81.

the court—namely, me! We jokingly composed a letter to the President to that effect—orally, and punctuated by giggles, squawks and guffaws. It was suggested that since [Democratic presidential candidate George] McGovern has publicly declared his first appointment to Supreme Court would be a woman, since President Nixon publicly stated that Senator Muskie's comment re Negro/Black V-P candidate was a "a libel on the American people," and since Nixon wants to win a second term in office, he could win brownie points by appointing the Pixie to fill Black's seat. We then concluded that, if by any miracle, this should happen the immediate result at Mass. General Hospital would be: "EMERGENCY: EMERGENCY: CALLING DR. HABER! CALLING DR. HABER—HEART ATTACK PATIENT IN EMERGENCY".

Meanwhile, on September 13, I was appointed the first Stulberg Professor of Law and Politics at Brandeis, a chair endowed by Louis Stulberg, President of the ILGWU [International Ladies' Garment Workers' Union]. So we said that simultaneously with the Brandeis announcement of my appointment would be an addendum that "Dr. M. was admitted to Mass. General Hosp. suffering from acute heart attack, etc. etc."

Then, I thought, I can't let my 18-yr.-old nephew aspire to the Presidency without myself making good on my joking comments of aspiration to the Supreme Court. It also seemed to be a good moment in history to present Mr. Nixon with a concrete example of what HE would do to avoid "a libel on the American people."

I slept on it, got up bright and early Saturday morning 9/18, and the attached first draft and also last draft is the result. It is perhaps the most unorthodox approach to a Supreme Court vacancy I can think of, but it has merit in that it would help to reduce the politics and shenanigans if the country would accept the idea that Supreme Court appointments, like CIVIL SERVICE, were handled on their merits, openly and without backroom politics. So I decided to gamble on the 200,000,000th chance and go for all the marbles. I do not want the history of the United States to record that Negro women of the 1970s had no high aspirations.

The upshot of all this is the attached. The developments are: last nite, 9/22, my letter was read to the Eastern Mass. Chapter of NOW, endorsed by the chapter and a coalition (very small) is in making to support my candidacy. Maida and Libby Koontz[5] are aware and will receive the document when the mails deliver tomorrow or Friday . . . It will be a gay old time with respect to Bundles From Boston to the White House!

Wish me luck—it seemed to me to be the right thing to do and I am relying on Divine Guidance in something as important as this. Perhaps, for just once in a lifetime, the rejections of the past will have steeled me not to care too much, or at least, to submerge personal ambitions in the larger issue—that of raising the issue without regard to the result.

All the best—and now to The American Legal System. Love

When her proposal caused hardly a ripple except among a handful of dedicated feminists, perhaps she realized that her quixotic plan was impossible; when the appointments of William Rehnquist as chief justice and Lewis Powell as associate justice are announced, she quickly turns to discussions about teaching. A course on women in 1971 put her among the pioneers teaching such courses.

⤴ Friday, October 22, 1971

5:15 a.m.

Dearest Skipper:

[. . .] Yesterday evening [. . .] I did not listen to the President's announcement of his nominees to the Supreme Court. (Mary Daly called and said two men were nominated but our conversation did not last long enough to get their identities.) [. . .] So I write this reaction with minimum prejudice against personalities.

First, in some ways I am relieved that this first stage has come to a conclusion [. . .]. We now move to Senate confirmation. This will allow me to shake free of outside interests and devote full time to my teaching responsibilities at Brandeis [. . .] my official registration for the American

5. Elizabeth Duncan Koontz (1919–89) was born and raised in North Carolina. She built an impressive career in education and was the first African American to head the National Education Association. She also worked with the Women's Bureau of the U.S. Labor Department and was a member of the North Carolina Commission on the Status of Women in 1963–64. She was highly respected by both Ware and Murray.

Legal System [. . .] is about 69 (about 40% or more women it appears.) In addition there are several "hitchhikers"—students who audit the class sessions. In order to improve my teaching techniques—by monitoring the class sessions—and to accommodate those students who cannot attend the first half-hour or the last half-hour of the course (because of conflicts in class schedules) we have begun to tape the class sessions [. . .] I have been listening to the tapes, making notes of issues I left up in the air or did not sufficiently clarify, or noting the extent to which the professor (me) dominated the discussion, etc. etc. It is a marvelous technique of self-evaluation. It also shows the limitation of taping, since the mike sits on the instructor's desk and picks up his/her words clearly but does not get as clear a recording of students' contributions, particularly those in the far corners of the room. [. . .]

The same practice has been introduced into the seminar on Women in American Life [. . .]. On the whole [. . .] I am modestly pleased with my performance. I can see *your* influence throughout—your use of episodes to illustrate points, your wide experience which encompasses many cultures and many people and forms a rich basis of material upon which to draw in widening the horizons of your students. [She goes on to describe several class sessions, some with visiting lecturers.]

All this is to say that school is beginning to be exciting, that I have gained some confidence as a teacher and that I do intend to make this, my "Senior" year at Brandeis, my very best year!

Another interesting (but confidential) item is that I have been asked to serve as Chairman of an Ad Hoc Tenure committee for reviewing the qualifications of a candidate to fill an endowed Chair on Christian Thought [. . .]. I accepted with the qualification that I was doing so primarily to know from the inside what the procedure is because I intend to promote reforms in the tenure system, and that my views on permitting an open hearing for candidates for tenure are a matter of public record. (See Valparaiso Law Review article). Did win this small concession: the Acting Dean of faculty has concurred in my view that the Committee may have the candidate appear in person before it, if necessary. [. . .]

This leads me back to the recent developments in re the issue of women on the Supreme Court. A few comments: [She argues that women of the country were taken by surprise (by her self-nomination) and if they had organized could have influenced the appointment. She suggests that women lawyers need to develop a talent pool of highly qualified women and then to promote articles about them so that they come to public attention. She is so fired up about the subject that she writes a blueprint for a Woman's Revolution (her term) that will, she believes, lead to the appointment of women to the Court in the near future.]

Ware's exciting early life experience had been with the denizens of the New Deal, so Joseph Lash's Eleanor and Franklin *reminds her of that time, when young reformers thought they could change the world—or at least the country.*

✈ 600 Beulah Road
Vienna, Virginia 22180
February 1, 1972
Dear Pixie:

What I neglected to say on the phone the other day was that I have been *living* "Eleanor and Franklin," to such a degree that I have hardly been in the present.[6] Of course, the first thing Gardiner did when the book came in was to look in the index and find you, so started with the good bits quoting your letters and poem. Then I settled in to a couple of chapters a night, and all the thoughts and memories they brought up, to live with the next day. One's feelings are on so many planes—how far we have come and how far we have *backslid*; how much more incredible Mrs. R. becomes as a person, the more one knows; how in the world did she ever manage to write so much to so many people (even you with your letter-writing propensity are dwarfed by the volume of her output), no matter how much she was doing or how fast she moved around; how on top of everything she managed to come to the rescue whenever family or friends were sick or in trouble; what an incredible number of people she managed to slip into the White House and to lunch or supper with Franklin, etc.etc; and FDR's longing for a light touch.

Pauline Coggs was here last week, as I think I mentioned. She recalled

6. Joseph Lash, *Eleanor and Franklin* (New York: W. W. Norton, 1971).

Mrs. R's saying she enjoyed being with her because she was just a person, whereas to be with Mrs. Bethune[7] was to be with a Cause! [. . .]

Cheerio! Skipper

Ware's furious remarks about the way the State Department had tried to use an African American woman, in the following letter, are typical of the way she views the world. Her young friend Mary Norris was in Boston for a while and briefly shared an apartment with Pauli Murray, whom she had come to know through Ware. The two had been together on Yellow Head Island and probably also at The Farm.

⇥ November 11, 1972

Dear Pixie—When my brother called from New Hampshire to say that they had 10 inches of snow, I thought I'd better hasten to mail you those boots of Mary Gresham's that have been sitting in the store room. They are on their way.

After talking yesterday with a member of the assembly of the Inter-American Commission of Women last month, I am even more upset than before over the way in which Jean (?) Cunningham was used. I already had the picture from some observations and from one of the South American delegates.

With no previous connection with the Commission, no knowledge of its operation history and in-fighting and no command of the language in which the Assembly was conducted, Spanish, she was appointed by the White House as chairman of the U.S. delegation—the host delegation— which involved presiding over the week-long meetings. She was appointed *solely because she was black.* In other words, she was put in an absolutely impossible position where she could not perform. I don't know who thought this one up, but it was as nasty a play as you can imagine:

1. It was a grave discourtesy to the guest delegations to appoint someone who did not speak the language. (Even with simultaneous translation you can't preside effectively over a sensitive political meeting [. . .])

7. Mary McLeod Bethune (1875–1955) was an educator and leader of the African American community who, among her many accomplishments, served FDR as special adviser on minority affairs.

2. To head the US delegation with someone who did not know the score was a fine way to express contempt for the women's bit and let all know that the US does not take its international role in this field seriously.

3. To put anyone in this situation is to crucify the individual who cannot be anything except a conspicuous failure; to pick a black woman for the role is to destroy her both as a person and as a symbol.

4. Libby Koontz was not even one of the ten or a dozen "advisers" in the US delegation (Catherine East [of the Women's Bureau in the Department of Labor] was). The competent and appropriate black woman who should have been there was pushed aside and excluded and a symbol imported.

Knowing that Latin Americans have their own kind of racial prejudices and their images of the US and its racial picture, you can see how many nasty angles this has.

Cunningham apparently handled herself with grace and dignity—the polite Latins and the US delegates that I spoke with commented that she was a lovely person—but she couldn't cope. She was neither able to keep the US straight on issues and out of the personal maneuvering and back-fighting going on in the Commission nor to handle the sessions where the back-fighting erupted. The Latins weren't sure whether the intent of the US government was to show contempt for them, for blacks, or for women in general—it was too obvious to be the result of accident, circumstance, indifference or even stupidity. My informants on the US delegation, who are sensitive people and Spanish speaking, said it was one of the most painful experiences of their lives. I haven't talked to Catherine East so don't know how she felt.

I write you about this because it represents such a cynical use of a fine woman for symbolic purposes and poses the problem of how to avoid being caught up and used this way in the climate of today. You may be running into Cunningham in the course of your doings and can maybe hear her version. Libby may also have an angle on the subject.

I am no longer involved in any way with the Inter-American Commission of Women, being *persona non grata* with the new administration there and the staff and being nowhere with the US official involvement. The Commission is a 100% mess, as far as that goes. What is hitting me here, for the moment, is not the bungling of Latin American relations but the abuse of a black woman as symbol—

I have missed Mary Norris's calls but Gardiner reports that she hasn't made it to Beacon Street as of a couple of nights ago—I trust that she gets out of the [illegible] trap soon. He said she was making some headway on the activity front. He is always vague in transmitting conversations, so I don't really know how things are working out there—

All the best—love Skipper.

THE

LAST

PHASE

After 1972 the correspondence slowed. Ware's eyes were giving her trouble and Murray was busy. There is plenty of evidence that they remained close and that Murray was often at The Farm. In 1973, after the death of her close friend and comrade Renee Barlow, Pauli decided to leave Brandeis and undertake training the for holy orders in the Episcopal Church.

Lina writes a long letter of support for Pauli's application to the General Theological Seminar and sends her a copy. She writes, in part:

[. . .] Pauli combines many qualities which make her not only a very exceptional but a most valuable candidate for the new career she hopes to enter. Her absolute integrity and total commitment mean that she will pour into her new activities all her very considerable abilities and wealth of varied experience, which cannot fail to enrich and inspire those with whom she comes in contact. As I have watched her through the years, I have seen her enter one area of activity after another, achieve the competence and excellence which would enable her to challenge complacencies and break out new frontiers, and then to offer constructive leadership [. . .]. She inspires people's confidence in themselves [. . .] and never misses an opportunity to call attention to those whose contributions might be overlooked. This she does with unfailing warmth and compassion, as well as a shrewd sense of what a person may need. [. . .]

Murray is accepted as a special student. In Song in a Weary Throat, *she says that the work at the seminary was much more demanding than anything she had encountered in law school. True to form, her journal includes much evidence of discontent with those in positions of authority at the seminary. She soon concluded that the seminary was organized for* young white men and was not hospitable to women or people of color. She writes some of her characteristic letters to the leaders of the institution. She herself says she soon had a reputation for being "abrasive," since—in her view—her tendency to probe and question was not welcome.

The battle of the women who had been allowed to take the training but were not immediately allowed ordination is dramatically told in Song. The women finally won the right after a turbulent meeting in Minneapolis in 1976.

The only letter I have seen—possibly the only one that survives—in which Murray, so to speak, talks back to Ware is on the letterhead of the General Theological Seminary and is marked in ink "Not Sent." They had apparently disagreed about Ernest Gaines's novel The Autobiography of Miss Jane Pittman or about Murray's castigation of a New York reviewer who denied that such people as Miss Jane Pittman could exist. Perhaps behind Murray's reaction is some pent up discontent with the fact that Ware still treats her as someone to be instructed. Early in their friendship when Pauli was an unknown law student, she had cast Lina in the role of guide and mentor. This was a role that came naturally to Ware and characterized her relationship with several young women besides Murray, such as Mary Norris, Dorothy Jackson, and Mary Gresham. Now Murray was a mature woman with considerable national stature, but the general tone of the relationship had not changed even though Ware admired Murray and went to extraordinary lengths to be helpful to her. She may have been unaware of just how "teacherly" she often was.

⤚ March 5, 1974 [Handwritten note:] Not Sent

Dearest Skipper:

I wish you trusted my judgment more about what I think is important. You and I do not always see eye to eye on such matters, but I am about as mature as I will ever be and therefore must make the final decision. I happen to think 'Miss Jane Pittman' is an extremely important event in the history of communication with respect to a problem we have wrestled with together as well as separately over more than thirty years. I also happen to think that I have a point of view which needs to be stated as often and as publicly as possible—because my goal is understanding, upon which reconciliation is based. I am not above a little self-promotion in the process. The enclosed copy of my letter to the Washington Post aims at all three. As Jenny Wren, Renee Barlow's mother would say, 'Now I've said it and I'm glad.'

Mary Norris testifies that when the two women were in the same place neither seemed reluctant to argue points of principle or strategy. There was, in person, less deference on the part of the younger woman than the letters appear to reflect.

The letters continue, at a slower pace, and are usually less concerned with public affairs than they had been in the past. In 1975 Murray's dissatisfaction with the General Theological Seminary prompted her to move to the Virginia Theological Seminary in Alexandria. In her application to the new seminary in 1975, she managed to be a bit flip. In answer to the question "Have you ever seen a physician regarding emotional or mental difficulties?" she wrote "Who hasn't" and went on to give as an example "writer's block 1952–53." There is no mention of her longtime concerns about her sexuality. Asked to list people who had been of special influence, she listed her family, especially Pauline Dame, Mrs. Roosevelt, Lloyd Garrison, Simon H. Rifkind, her "beloved friend and Episcopalian colleague Irene Barlow, Leon Ransom, Judge William Hastie, and Thomas Emerson." She named Ware and Means as the "most continuous intellectual influence" on her life.

Lina Ware writes from Yellow Head to say that she left groceries in Pauli's new apartment in Alexandria and, as usual, urges her to come to the island if she has time and energy.

On Thanksgiving Day 1975 Pauli joins Lina, Gardiner, Mary Norris, and Mary's mother, Craig, for dinner. Writing a mutual friend about the dinner, Pauli says: "They seem in good health but they are frail and I regretted having to leave them."

In 1976, as she finishes her training, she and Lina discuss what her future in the church should be. She is worried about her health and suffering some anxiety. They agree that she should not undertake a regular parish. Pauli's journal records her search for divine guidance— and her loneliness. She speaks of needing companionship, which has been absent since Renee's death.

The invitation to Yellow Head is repeated the following year, and in 1977 a postcard arrives, still in Ware's handwriting, though a bit more difficult to read:

Needless to say all its [the island's] occupants miss you. Mary & Joyce plucked us off the plane at Bangor and provided us with a couple of ravishing blue days. Now it is foggy and rain again—cool and relaxing. Everyone already feeling renewal. Wish you were here too. All send love, Skipper and Co.

A woman, and a black woman at that, ordained an Episcopal priest was news indeed. The Reverend Peter Lee, minister of the Chapel of the Cross in Chapel Hill, heard about Murray and invited her to celebrate her first Eucharist in that church, where her grandmother had been baptized as one of "five servant children belonging to Miss Mary Smith." Lee was in touch with CBS News reporter Charles Kuralt, who came with his camera to create an episode for his long-running "On the Road" program. Pauli was impressive in the service and charming in her interview with Kuralt. Watching it on videotape, I thought it showed the spirit that led to her numerous friendships.

In August 1977 Pauli writes to Lina about that Eucharist and being interviewed by Kuralt. She writes, too, about her ongoing effort to write an autobiography. On August 16 Lina thanks her for a birthday card and sends along some of Hilda Smith's poems. A year later Lina's letter is all local news, about friends visiting and an outboard motor causing trouble. As is by now customary, she urges Pauli to come to Yellow Head, but Murray is finding travel more and more difficult.

Though she describes herself to Kuralt as full of energy, Murray did not feel quite up to coping with a full-time parish appointment, so she served several churches in Maryland and the District of Columbia part time, delivered many sermons, and spoke to gatherings of young women around the country, usually to an enthusiastic response.

On August 28, 1978, Murray writes about a paperback edition of Proud Shoes, *and reports that she has fifty pages written on the new book. She reports being in touch with Hilda Smith, who had just turned ninety—Lina had brought them together many years before.*

One more conflict with the University of North Carolina was still to come. In 1978 Murray was invited to receive an honorary degree from the institution that had, not so long ago, rejected her application for admission. She was at first delighted, and accepted the invitation. Then she discovered that the university was locked in combat with the federal Department of Health, Education, and Welfare over the issue of expanding the number of black students. Governor James B. Hunt Jr. supported the university's unwillingness to comply with an HEW order.

Murray's reaction was to work out a proposal for mediation of the conflict, which she sent to all the concerned parties from the governor of the state down, along with a list of possible mediators, most of whom would have been likely to side with HEW. She made her suggestion in an open letter. It was politely received, but none of the recipients agreed to anything of the sort. While she waited for a resolution, Murray wrote to Virginia Dunlap at the university that if the honorary degree citation included the fact that she was the granddaughter of a slave it must also include the fact that she was the great-granddaughter of a slave owner!

When the UNC-HEW situation is not resolved, Pauli decides that under the circumstances she cannot share a platform with Governor Hunt, who had not only defied HEW, but also had refused to pardon civil rights activists in Wilmington, North Carolina—the so-called Wilmington Ten—who had been convicted (the convictions were subsequently overturned) of fire-bombing a convenience store. She reluctantly withdraws her acceptance of the honor.

On August 13, 1979, Murray congratulates Ware on her eightieth birthday and reports that she is weary after performing two weddings in one day. The experience convinces her of the wisdom of her decision not to take on a regular parish.

In 1979 the annual Ware-Means Christmas report deplores the state of the country, saying there is nothing to do but hold on. Lina and Gardiner are delighted with the response to their gift of fifty acres of The Farm to the state of Virginia for a permanent park (the rest to be added on their death). There had been a celebration of this magnificent gift at The Farm, and Pauli Murray had given the invocation.

On February 19, 1981, responding to a request from Pauli in the interest of her autobiography, Lina writes a long letter recounting an episode early in their friendship when a group of young women from Howard, after a picnic at The Farm, had taken a bus back to Washington, and some of them had refused to move to the back. They were put in jail, and Lina bailed them out. She recalled their enthusiasm:

At the jail I found the students in high spirits. They did not think that I would be able to raise bail on a Sunday afternoon, so were bent on making themselves as comfortable as possible for the night. They asked for towels. One girl had sore feet and requested medication. They made up a song about the Fairfax county jail—all to the tune of the Leadbelly Boll Weevil song which we had been playing on the victrola at the Farm and they sang it lustily to the entertainment of inmates and prison guards alike . . . [She adds that, once out on bail, their chief worry was about being late back to the dormitory.]

The case went to trial, where it was handled by one or more NAACP lawyers [. . .]. The judgment against the students was automatic [. . .]. The case was appealed. On the way back to town we circled the Lincoln Memorial and paused in front of the steps to wave to the statue of Lincoln and call out "Abe Here we are, still at it."

The case was appealed to the Virginia state supreme court and a date set but before it came time to go to trial, the state withdrew the charge and the case was dropped [. . .]. The students and we were disappointed, for they had hoped to be the test case by which jim crow would be thrown out [. . .].

Skipper

A brief handwritten note on Three Kings Day in 1981 is the last in Ware's own hand. When her sight grows so dim that she cannot write, she dictates. As long as Lina is in Maine, Murray sends up all sorts of clippings as well as tapes full of Washington news. Though they are in different places, she says that she and Lina and Maida are enjoying reading together about women in the labor movement.

Sometime in the 1980s Maida had moved to Pittsburgh to be near Eric and his family, living in one half of a duplex. Toward the end of her life Pauli came to live in the other half. She continued to work on her autobiography and for the Episcopal Church.

In November 1984 Lina writes about the death of Patricia Harris, who had been her student and a good friend of Pauli's. She also sends along three possible prefaces for what would become Song in a Weary Throat. *Not long after, Murray was diagnosed with pancreatic cancer, and on July 1, 1985, she died in the house in Pittsburgh. On July 5 a memorial service was held in the National Cathedral in Washington.*

Ware is becoming increasingly frail. She continues to follow the process by which Murray's final work is being edited for publication and writes four drafts of a proposed introduction. None was accepted by the publisher, but she is asked to write an epilogue. She writes, in part:

All who knew Pauli were impressed by the tremendous energy that drove her to achieve excellence in everything she undertook. They felt her total commitment, a commitment that made her always ready to use herself as an instrument to advance whatever cause she was pursuing. They saw her stand firm on principle, pressing through confrontation toward reconciliation by means of reason and disciplined nonviolence. Already she has become a symbol and guiding light to many who never had the privilege of knowing her personally. [. . .] To be treated as a human being and to regard all others as members of the same human family were at the core of Pauli's outlook and effort. As she prefaced her book of poems, Dark Testament:

I speak for my race and my people—
The human race and just people.

This is her legacy.

In March 1986, several groups at the University of North Carolina at Chapel Hill sponsor a symposium entitled "Black Women's Leadership: Challenges and Strategies" dedicated to the memory of "the Late Reverend Doctor Pauli Murray." Maida Springer is the first speaker, and Eleanor Holmes Norton gives the keynote address. Maida had made sure to bring Lina on this pilgrimage to Chapel Hill to honor Pauli. She was almost totally blind and very thin. I was lucky enough to dine with the two of them, and made a note in my journal about my longtime friend:

She is blind—can't read—has some trouble signing her name. She is painfully thin and hardly tasted her supper, barely finished a small glass of beer. Has she lost her taste for food, I wonder? Her mind is clear, her memory excellent—still has the habit (as she did twenty years ago and maybe all her life) of telling stories with much detail. Her warm friendships all her life stand her in good stead now that she is in need of some help to do most anything. She is still very spry except of course she is uncertain: where are the steps? That sort of thing. She told me that when she was young she would have thought she didn't want to live impaired but that when you get there you make the most of what you have. Still, I wonder—I would fear just

*becoming depressed. She is a remarkable person and has written bits
and pieces of her autobiography. I wish I had time to try to pull it all
together and get the rest out of her: how she came to be such an em-
blematic new woman. Lucky to have married one of the most interesting of men.*

How I now regret not following that impulse to "get the rest out of
her" and, indeed, not asking where the "bits and pieces of autobiography" are to be found.

Two years later Gardiner died, and in due course Lina moved to
Collington, an Episcopal retirement community in Maryland. Her final
Christmas letter sent in 1989 sounds many familiar notes as she urges
friends to take the Orange Metro Line out from Washington and come
visiting:

Visits from many good friends have been a source of pleasure, and I
dearly hope these will continue. Please satisfy this hope in the New Year.
Lina Ware.

In 1990 she died in her sleep, a few months short of her ninetieth birthday.

In 1922 Caroline Ware was a student at Oxford. This letter, to her close friend Helen Lockwood (from the Lockwood Papers, Special Collections, Vassar College Libraries), provides a snapshot of the young Caroline Ware and foreshadows the adult Ware very well.

→{ St. Giles, Oxford, October 16, 1922

Dear Helen:

[...] Life at Oxford takes shape. Today I experienced my first class and my first introduction to the excruciating politeness and utter silence of the Oxford undergraduate as far as the "lady student" is concerned. One of the rules we have for our delectation says, "Conversation with men undergraduates before and after lectures is not encouraged." It is not. Professor Firth was scheduled to hold a class this morning at Oriel College. The omniscient porter to whom one applies for everything directed me to lecture room no. 4. I went. The room, in fact the whole hall, was quite empty. I sat. After a time a man in a B.A. gown came in and sat also. We waited. Said he, "Prof. Firth begins his lectures today, does he not?" We looked it up to be sure, and continued to wait. Some minutes later he observed, "He doesn't speak very loud, we had better sit on the other side of the room." We did. We waited. Subsequently he remarked, "He is a very scholarly old gentlemen. He doesn't attract many people." We waited. At about fifteen minutes past the hour a man who might have been a porter came in and suggested that we might find Professor Firth in his room. We went, the B.A. competently leading the way, I trailing behind. Sure enough he was in his room, one with a stone mantel and portraits upon the wall, presiding at the head of a big old mahogany table over four men. The B.A. stepped back and let me in first. The class was most entertaining but the only gleam of humor that I caught in anyone's eye was a twinkle from a Harvard man. The Englishmen all maintained a stolid solemnity. After about half an hour, Prof. Firth said, "I don't want to keep anyone." Nobody moved, so I sat tight, and conversation about Tudor foreign policy and the stupidity of the officials of the Public Record office continued in a desultory fashion. After awhile Prof. Firth said again "I don't want to keep anybody. Of course I am ready to answer any questions or discuss anything." This time two of the others got up, so I rose too and made towards the door. Whereat Prof. Firth observed, "I don't want to drive you out. I'm quite at anybody's service for another hour and a quarter." The others edged back a bit, so I edged too. Finally one of the men got as far as the door, with me at his heels. Whereat he opened the door and stood back with the most polite air while I went out. But when I turned to thank him and to make some remarks on the class, he was gone in stark silence, streaking down the corridor in the opposite direction. Such is Oxford!

I do like it though, no end, in spite of the utterly absurd rules and regulations that make you feel like an infant or an idiot and the fact that one has to go about hindered by the wearing of a highly inadequate gown and inoffensive cap, without which one may not attend lectures or university sermons, appear before an officer of the university, and venture into the Bodleian, an examination, or the streets at night. I suffered a few moments of discouragement when the old lady of the house came home, especially as her daughter kindly warned me that it was not safe to oppose her by expressing any unorthodox views on religion, politics, economics, war, imperialism, ghosts—anything one might have a view on, in fact. She is a total fool, and gets disgustingly sentimental over the dogs, and talks with a sort of pride about the "very bad districts" in which she sometimes goes to visit people and is on the whole quite intolerable, but silence at meals can be endured, and the English students in the house, as well as the old dame's daughter, are excellent. I find myself, however, pouncing with glee upon stray Americans because you can't laugh with English people over characteristically English things for they aren't of course, funny to them, and I continue to be unspeakably amused at their ways. They are so pathetically appreciative of this stretch of good weather, warm days, cloudless skies, and balmy, star-lit nights. Even the laconic B.A. had something to say about that.

One of the prime joys of the place arises from the little villages which surround the town. So far I have discovered three within a couple of miles of my abode, each more picturesque than the others, each with an entrancing old church and sweet little churchyard containing worn old stones, yew trees, and countless English robins. I don't suppose English village life has much to recommend it but the looks of the villages are decidedly in their favor.

[She finishes with advice about a place to visit in Paris.] Lina

---

In 1938 Pauli Murray applied for admission to do graduate work at the University of North Carolina. The following exchange of letters between Murray and Frank Porter Graham, president of the university, bolsters the image conjured up by her statement that one woman with a typewriter is a social movement.

225 W. 110 street
Apartment 5
New York, N.Y.
January 17, 1939
Dr. Frank P. Graham
University of North Carolina
Chapel Hill, N.C.
Dear Sir:

I have followed with interest the various activities and statements which have grown out of the issue of admitting Negroes to the University of North Carolina.

Now that the air has cleared a bit, may I present a point of view which I believe warrants some consideration? First, let me say that despite the legal implications of this controversy, which as you say, rest in the hands of the State and its courts, I have no desire to stir up racial conflict or student antagonism on the campus. That would be unwise on the part of any prospective student.

Secondly, as you must know from the date of my application, I knew nothing of the Lloyd Gaines case at the time I applied. I did know, however, of Thomas Hocutt's attempt to enter your school of Pharmacy some three or more years ago. From my conversations with him, I gained the impression that he was rejected on the grounds that his educational qualifications made him ineligible to enter the university. Hocutt received his undergraduate training in a Negro college of North Carolina.

This very fact reinforces the assertion that Negro schools in North Carolina have not been given those facilities which will place them on a par with white schools. Furthermore, accepting your premise that further segregation in the graduate schools is a "wise long-range solution," what guarantee have the Negro students of North Carolina that their graduate facilities will be any higher in quality than their undergraduate schools? My personal contacts with other Negro students who have come to Northern colleges for their graduate work, on the basis of their own admissions, has led me to believe that their undergraduate work was so inadequate, that it was necessary for them to take additional courses or remain in school a longer period of time to supply this deficiency.

What some members of your school have failed to realize are the following facts:

1. I am particularly interested in the Public Welfare and Social Science Departments of your school. This interest was stimulated by my visit to this department in the spring of 1934 and through my contact with the publications which have come from this department.

2. That your Social Science Department has developed a series of courses which are basic to any understanding of the social, economic and racial problems of the South, and the names of Professors [Guy] Johnson and [Howard] Odum rank high in the field of sociology for their contributions to literature on these problems; that they naturally attract serious-minded students who are interested in this particular phase of American life.

3. That I am well aware of the difficulties and problems which will confront any inter-racial undertaking south of the Mason-and-Dixon line, that I can appreciate the psychological conflicts which would arise in the minds of a group of students faced with a sudden departure from a traditional policy of racial segregation, but that I believe this problem can be met through frank, open discussion by representatives of both groups. I conceive of a give-and-take process where prejudices are openly aired and accounted for, where correct interpretations are made and where enlightenment is gained in an atmosphere of mutual cooperation and respect.

4. That even if the University does admit negro students, the qualifications required will eliminate those Negro applicants who have not reached the same educational and intellectual development of the students already present at the school. Such Negro students, it

seems to me, would have a definite contribution to make to inter-racial understanding and good will.

5. That the majority of thinking Negroes regard, with skepticism, the recommendation of "equal graduate schools for Negroes in North Carolina," that they consider it an evasion on the part of Southern white leaders and a strengthening of the bars of racial inequality. That while the majority of Negroes are no more anxious to mix socially with whites than the whites are with Negroes, they right-fully resent any law which prohibits their admittance to any public institution of learning because of race.

6. That although many Negroes remain silent and tactful in the pres-ence of whites, any "idealist" pressing for the logical consequences of the democratic concept of "equal rights" is merely articulating the unexpressed, unrevealed desires and sentiments of the group which he represents.

7. That the opinion which I express here and in all other statements, flows directly from my great desire to get at the bottom of those racial prejudices which so inhibit the development of human be-ings, whether they be white or black. That I left the South to try to find the answer, but the enlightenment gained here is not enough; that the answer to some of my question lies in the hearts and minds and intelligence of southern whites as well as in ourselves, and there is no better place to find some of these answers than in an institution of higher learning with a tradition of liberal thought.

Finally, since the recent poll conducted at your University indicates an active student interest in this problem, would there be any place in your school program to conduct a discussion at which some of the following questions could be raised for study? (The same experiment was tried out at Harvard University some years ago on the question of Jewish students. I am sure many Negro students all over the country would appreciate knowing the findings of such a discussion.)

1. What is "social equality"? Is "social equality" the same as "ra-cial equality"? Is an inter-racial conference an expression of social equality?

2. Does the concept of democracy include equal rights for minority groups?

3. To what extent would the admission of a Negro student to the University of North Carolina affect the prestige of the school?
4. What advantages might be gained, if any, through admitting a Negro student to classes? What disadvantages?
5. If the purposes of higher education are to gain insight into social problems, what valid objections would white students have in admitting a Negro student to their classes?
6. To what extent would white students be able to discuss Negroes frankly if a Negro were present in their classes?
   What conduct would white students expect on the part of a Negro student on the campus?
7. If the students of the University of North Carolina are convinced that it is unjust, unwise and dictatorial to admit a Negro student into their classes, by what means can they test this theory in real life if they have not had the experience of a negro student on the campus?
8. What have been the experiences of Southern white students in Northern universities where they found Negro students? Have these students left school? Has the presence of Negroes in their classes hampered their ability to learn?
9. What has been the experience of the athletic teams of the University of North Carolina in playing those schools having a Negro on the team? Has it been distasteful? Has it been successful? If successful, can the spirit of fair play evidenced on the foot-ball field be transferred to the classroom and with what degree of success?
10. Would it be possible to get any student opinion on these questions?
    Yours very truly,
    Pauli Murray

Copies to:
The Tar Heel
University of N.C.
The Durham Morning Herald
Durham, N.C.
The Carolina Times
Durham, N.C.

President Graham replied

→ Miss Pauli Murray
225 W. 110 Street
Apartment 5
New York City
My dear Miss Murray:

I wish to thank you for your letter and the spirit which runs through it. I have been on a night and day schedule in connection with the proposed budget for the University of North Carolina, which, if carried through would heavily damage this institution. I am just now taking time off from the legislative sessions to catch up with my correspondence.

I am aware of the inequities which you point out. Many months before the Gaines decision, the wise Governor of the state appointed a Commission to study the whole question of Negro education in general and professional and graduate work for Negroes in North Carolina. This Commission, of which ex-Senator Noel of Person County is chairman, and Mr. N. C. Newbold is secretary, has made its report and the Legislature has set up a committee to consider the recommendations made in the report of the Governor's Commission. This Committee, in a very serious way, is now considering the whole question of graduate and professional work for Negroes in North Carolina as a clear responsibility of the Legislature of the state. Mr. Victor S. Bryant, representative from Durham County, is chairman of the committee considering the matter for the Legislature. Mr. Walter Murphy, of Rowen, as a member of Mr. Bryant's committee, is working on a bill with Mr. Bryant. The legislature will make its decision within the next month or six weeks. The legislative committee, as I understand it, is taking into account the following facts:

1. The provision in the Constitution of North Carolina requiring the separation of the races in public education.

2. The decision of the Supreme Court that the state must make substantially equal provision for graduate and professional work in the separate Negro institutions or admit Negroes to the state university;

3. The Constitution of the State prevails up to the point where it is overruled by the Constitution of the United States as interpreted by the Supreme Court;

4. The only way to obey both the state Constitution and the United

States Constitution is to make adequate provision in the separate Negro institutions;

5. If the state Constitution is not over-ruled by the United States Constitution then the only way to change a provision in the state Constitution is by referendum of the people.

The Negro leaders in this state and the white leaders who have been friends of the Negroes in the struggle for justice are strongly of the opinion that the most unfortunate thing that could happen at this time would be a popular referendum on the race issue. The possibilities of an inter-racial throwback do not have to be emphasized in the present world.

The hundred years progress of the Southern Negro is perhaps without parallel in history. A study of the advances made by North Carolina toward more equal provision for Negroes in the public school and in the state colleges is encouraging. A comparison of appropriations both for maintenance and for buildings clearly shows that we are moving ahead in North Carolina in this very basic matter of fairer treatment of our Negro fellow citizens. We must move forward. We must not be unwise in the present critical situation and cause a throwback to a darker time with losses all along the line. It is the millions who suffer in such a throwback.

You realize that inter-racial inequalities are not confined to the Southern part of the United States. In the northern universities, though not under prohibition of the law, there are, I understand, no Negro professors. It seems that the only career open to the Negro professor in institutions of higher learning is in the Negro colleges of the South.

Taking account of the Constitution of North Carolina, the decision of the United States Supreme Court and the clear intent of the Legislature of North Carolina I have pledged as far as my lawful responsibility permits, the cooperation of the University of North Carolina with the North Carolina College for Negroes and the North Carolina Agricultural and Technical College for Negroes toward a more adequate provision for Negroes in the public schools, higher standard Negro undergraduate colleges, and a substantial beginning in the provision of graduate and professional work. This may seem to you to be an inadequate and minimum program, but it is going to take the cooperation and the struggle of all to bring it to pass. The present alternative is a throwback against whose consequences we must unceasingly be on guard in the best interest of both races, who after all go up or down together.

As you may know, I am under very bitter attack in some parts of North Carolina and the lower South for what little I have tried to do in behalf of Negro people, organized and unorganized workers and other underprivileged groups. I realize that I am also subject to attack because I understand the limitations under which we must work in order to make the next possible advances.

With kindest regards to you, I am

Sincerely yours,

Frank P. Graham

President.

Pauli Murray was not admitted to the University of North Carolina. However, a few years later she invited Frank Porter Graham to join in something called National Sharecroppers Week, with which she was associated, and he agreed. He also wrote, at her request, a preface to a pamphlet about the Odell Waller case for the Workers Defense League. While she never deviated from her belief that the university must admit African American students (which it began to do more than a dozen years after her application, in the 1950s), she understood the pressures under which President Graham worked and admired his achievements in that context. Lina Ware also spoke of Graham as a good friend.

What, my friends ask with some insistence: what did you learn from this enterprise? The answer is: a great deal that I did not guess at the outset. Yet, in the end I am left with many questions.

About Pauli Murray and her forty-three-year friendship with Lina Ware, I had everything to learn. As I re-read Murray's two autobiographies and read and re-read the extraordinary correspondence between the two women, I realized more and more the challenge it is for any outsider to understand what it means to be black in American society. Extraordinary though Murray was, her life was shaped by her acute sensitivity, first to segregation and then to numerous other discriminations to which all people of color were subject. She felt a need to deal with every case of injustice that came to her attention.

Her life was also shaped by uncertainties about her sexual nature and fears of hereditary insanity. She herself speculated that these "terrors" had something to do with her energy for protest. Combined with her high intelligence and her insatiable ambition for achievement and recognition, the fears somehow also contributed to her almost endless capacity for hard work. Doubtless they also had something to do with the volatility of her spirit.

All that is only part of the story. Many people testify to Murray's charm and warmth, indeed to her magnetism. When she lectured to diverse audiences, she was often able to endear herself to whole groups of people. She did great kindnesses for friends who were in trouble or unhappy. She had a constant concern for Maida Springer's well-being. She gave money she could not afford when friends needed help. At the same time, she could move from unusual self-confidence to devastating self-analysis in a single day.

She was out front on issues that later became central to the great national movement for civil rights. Her challenges to the University of North Carolina, to the courts in the Waller case, to Washington restaurants, to the state of Virginia in the bus incident, to Cornell University, and to any individual or group she perceived as discriminating against

African Americans prefigured the more familiar challenges of the 1960s. The energy and time she devoted to challenging every example of discrimination she observed are astounding.

Her letters, and even more her journal notes, reveal a complex inner life. The public persona, depicted in many of her letters and in her autobiographical writing, was quite different from the private one. She had a hard time working at the direction of another person, many times seething in private while in public doing a fine job. She was hypersensitive to slights, yet could examine her own failings. Letter writing was often therapy.

My husband, Andrew Scott, who was until his death a collaborator in most of my scholarly endeavors, read the correspondence between Lina Ware, whom he knew, and Pauli Murray, whose books he had read, and offered the following observations:

> Hers [Murray's] was a passionate voice, an angry voice, sometimes an imploring voice as she called on her nation to complete its work, to live up to its principles . . . Was she often hard to have around? Believe it. If you didn't accept her position she would want to know why. If you did accept them, why were you not out there protesting as she was? Pauli was not your quiet do-gooder. She would not let you go to church on Sunday and live a normal life the other six days. She wanted you to be out there every day.

He described the hurdles that faced her as a woman and a black woman and then went on:

> She might plead "I am human. I demand justice and equality." But the answer would come back: "My dear, you are human to be sure, but you are a black, female human." . . . Pauli was a warrior. She fought for changes all her life and effectively. But, paradoxically, she was vulnerable and uncertain inwardly . . . Anyone who wants to understand her must see her as a warrior whose own, internal fortifications were often shaky . . .

I think he had it right.

About Caroline Ware I came to learn more than our friendship, intermittent visits, and joint efforts on behalf of women had revealed. In retrospect I realize how little she talked about herself: we always seemed to talk about history, or public affairs, or farming, or Maine and Nova Scotia. I knew of course that she was an innovative historian whose *Cultural Approach to History* had pointed the way to a future not then envisioned by many students of the American past. I knew about her work on the status of women, and I knew that she raised Sheltie dogs. But there was much more to learn.

A foray into her papers at the FDR Library in Hyde Park revealed the extraordinary number of other things in which she was deeply involved. From undergraduate days Ware had been a historian who believed that scholarship should lead to action, so it was not surprising that she was attracted to worker education, which became a lifelong commitment. (Now I understood why she had taken me on a pilgrimage to meet Hilda Smith, still working in her eighties.)

Then came the somewhat accidental job as a consumer advocate that also turned in to a lifelong commitment. When she joined the Howard School of Social Work, she found herself teaching students about community organization, an interest that she carried first to Puerto Rico and then to nearly every country in Latin America. Her book on that subject, published in Spanish, was in print for a very long time, and her connection with that part of the world continued until the end of her life.

How did a historian with a Harvard Ph.D. come to make social action so central a part of her life, and public advocacy so central a means to make a difference? She answered that question in 1967 when the Radcliffe Alumnae Association awarded her its Graduate Medal. She wanted, she told the group, to find something to say that would have meaning for those who, "like me, find scholarship and action inextricably intertwined." She found unity in her many different activities in

[. . .] the processes by which people become active and responsible participants in the life of their societies, not passive onlookers, victims or beneficiaries of the decisions and manipulations of others. The great tendency of this century has been just this—the fuller participation as active and responsible members of their communities and nation of more and more kinds of people who, through past centuries, furnished the passive base for the wealth and culture they did not share. [. . .] We hear much today of the revolution of rising expectations. The counterpart is the revolution of rising participation [. . .].

Ware believed that all the disparate pieces of her career were concerned with making that revolution of rising participation a reality. To that end, she worked hard to develop effective voluntary associations both in the United States and in Latin America. Also to that end, she devoted much energy to an effort to make equality a reality for all Americans. Her optimism was tested a good many times, there were even moments of despair, but she never gave up. In every endeavor she demonstrated unusual competence.

Lina Ware was not much interested in material possessions, but she cared deeply about ideas, and she cultivated people she thought were trying to get to the root of things. Her own mode of thought was inductive. From close observation she built up her ideas about the subject at hand, with the result that her analysis tended to be revealed through one story after another, stories that were not simply decorative but were an important part of her fundamental way of thinking.

Her professional career was shaped by the prevailing prejudice against women scholars. She did not often rail against that prejudice, but when she came upon a specific example, as she had in the National Defense Advisory Commission, she was prepared to fight. The quality of her historical scholarship overcame the normal prejudices in a male-dominated profession, though when it came to academic posts, the prejudices still held. Teaching at Vassar in her youth, she had hoped for a chance at a university. A summer job at the University of Wyoming was abruptly canceled when those who had hired her discovered that she was married, and later she was told by a member of the University of Maryland history department that a woman would not be considered for a post there. Still, she said, she found great compensations in her experience at Howard.

The Ware-Means marriage was as equal as any of her generation, though there were moments when she questioned whether maintaining the double role of spouse and scholar was worth the stress it brought. Those moments evaporated. She and Gardiner Means were partners in work as well as in marriage, and remained so in their eighties, when he was deaf and she was blind. She fretted that he would never finish his magnum opus that was to have pushed Keynes off the stage—and she was right, he never did. But more than most couples they maintained their strong sense of partnership as long as they lived.

Ware's view of American politics and government was shaped by the early New Deal and by her experience as a lobbyist. In her eighties she puzzled about the fact that many New Dealers had run out of energy and enthusiasm by 1937 and wondered why her admired Puerto Ricans, with many fewer resources, could maintain *their* energy over a much longer span.

She was a natural "networker," and she liked concrete problems. She was a small "d" democrat and was suspicious of anybody who thought he or she knew what was good for other people—unless that person was herself.

Ware's intelligence, diligence, generosity, and goodwill are beyond doubt—but is this all that can be said? Was there some not-well-understood complexity concealed by her open, straightforward manner? In spite of her concern for other people not like herself—women workers, African Americans, Puerto Rican peasants, Latin Americans generally, young Germans—she remained a New Englander. Though she lived in Virginia for fifty-seven of her ninety years, and gave her beloved farm to be a park for Virginians in perpetuity, it was never quite "home," "for the pines and birches [of New England] are my country," she wrote Pauli in 1954.

Finally, despite her open-hearted, friendly spirit, there was an element of restraint, of privacy, evident in the fact that she carefully preserved the record of her public life but kept very few documents that might have illuminated her private life. In the study of any human life some mysteries are never solved.

The relationship between Ware and Murray changed a little as the two women grew older, as Pauli matured and became a national figure, and as both were disillusioned by the domestic and foreign policies of the United States government. Early in their friendship, Murray cast Ware in the role of mentor and gave her extravagant credit for what she, Pauli, was doing. There can be no question of Ware's high regard for Murray, or of her steady helpfulness in so many ways, including financial help. At the same time, she did not reject the nickname of "Skipper" for herself or the diminutive "Pixie" for her friend. As for Murray, she seemed to delight in being a "pixie," whatever that meant to her.

Ware assumed the right to give advice, though she seldom asked for any. Over time her letters became more didactic and perhaps a shade less diplomatic. On the other hand her epilogue to *Song in a Weary Throat*, written after Murray's death, conveyed undiminished admiration.

Pauli, for her part, became a little restive as they both aged, as evidenced by her disagreement with Lina in regard to *The Autobiography of Miss Jane Pittman*. This was a small controversy, however, not significant in the larger picture. Pauli's profound affection for Lina is evident in the steady stream of clippings and news and postcards she sent to Maine or to Virginia as Lina grew older.

Mary Norris, who knew both women and often saw them together, observed that Ware's relationship with Pauli was very important to them both, but that it was a relationship between people whose life circumstance could not have been more different, so it was not a simple peer friendship. As Norris explains,

> I don't mean Lina looked down in some way from lofty heights—she would never have felt better or more august than Pauli. She just had a deep confidence in herself and played the teacher or mentor or listener or supporter role in most of what she did with virtually everyone. She was very open to all authentic experiences and drew many lessons from them, but she was able to do all that because she was very secure in who she was as a person [. . .]. Lina did all her amazing things as a natural flow from her essential self-security [. . .] while Pauli did all her amazing things with almost none of that security, with a constant worry that she had hereditary madness, with all the slings and arrows of racism, with terrible fears flowing from her childhood [. . .] with terrible self-doubts and difficulties about her sexuality, and with a constant financial struggle. During the time I lived with Pauli, I couldn't imagine how she had put one foot after the other from day to day, let alone became a leader in civil and gender rights and in so many other ways.[1]

1. Personal letter, February 2004, in my possession.

I think Norris is perceptive.

Readers will decide for themselves what to read into words, phrases, exchanges of thought, nicknames. They may ask why Ware was willing to spend so much time—time upon which so many had a claim—working on Murray's manuscripts. How did the two friends manage not to let Murray's need for money shape their relationship? It does not appear to have done so. Did the two talk about Murray's struggles with issues of sexuality? There are hints that they did, but not of Lina's reaction. And so on.

Reading what these two wrote about the burning issues of their time reminds me how much we are all creatures of the context in which we live and work, and how differently some events are viewed by historians from the way they were perceived at the time. I am especially struck by the optimism they usually exhibited that the world could indeed be made better—in contrast to the pervasive pessimism of our day.

It was the fate of these women to strive for change separately and in support of each other decades before the large national movements for civil rights and gender rights took shape. Both had public careers in the middle decades of the twentieth century. Caroline Ware fought most of her battles from inside powerful institutions, where she managed to change agendas. Pauli Murray, for the most part, was an outsider forcing attention to issues of race and gender that most Americans preferred to leave untouched. Ware appreciated the dimensions of what Murray was trying to do and the fact that in that battle, despite her profound self-criticism, "Pixie" never flinched. Murray valued her Brahmin ally as one wise, well connected, and always there when she needed help of many kinds.

Each made a difference, expanding the universe of those included in her circle of concern. Had they been able to work for another decade they might have been recognized by members of the movements that followed as forebears and pacesetters who make the point that the status quo wouldn't do. Their incremental gains, achieved in part through the staunch support they gave each other, set the stage for the great leaps forward that came in the second half of the twentieth century.

These selections from their correspondence bring two remarkable women into the light of our day and back to the center of their times. Both Pauli Murray and Caroline Ware led lives in which ideas and action were "inextricably intertwined." Both rejected the role of "passive onlookers, victims or beneficiaries of the decisions and manipulations of others." In revealing lives of informed public engagement, fearless protest, concern for others, and steadfast mutual support, their correspondence speaks to the needs of our time was well as theirs.

→{ ACKNOWLEDGMENTS

The "community of scholars" is not an idle phrase, nor is the idea of a circle of friends. Without both I would not have made it.

Three people were present at the creation: Susan Ware, Linda Kerber, and Nancy Cott. Susan stayed with the project from start to finish, going far beyond the call of friendship.

Early on, members of the staff at the Schlesinger Library of the Radcliffe Institute for Advanced Study in Cambridge, Massachusetts, were indispensable. Jaclyn Blume, Sarah Hutcheon, Jane Knowles, Kathy Jacobs, Kathy Kraft, Anne Englehart, and Laurie Ellis constituted ever-present help.

Dean Rogers at the Vassar College Library and Robert Clark and his colleagues at the Franklin D. Roosevelt Library in Hyde Park, New York, were repeatedly helpful.

As the book developed, many historians joined the party: Glenda Gilmore, Davison Douglas, John Demos, Pat and Loren Graham, Jacquelyn Hall, Suzanne Lebsock, Sydney Nathans, Elizabeth Payne, Rosalind Rosenberg, Peter Wallenstein, Nancy Weiss, Burt Malkiel, and Rebecca Scott did their best to keep me on the straight and narrow.

Dara DeHaven educated me about the court decisions that so fascinated Pauli Murray. Ken Rutherford also took a lawyer's look at part of the manuscript. Michael O'Leary was a steady help in Cambridge.

Two people who knew both the protagonists well had information to be found nowhere else: Mary Norris and Peggy McIntosh took time from their very busy lives to talk to me over and over, and to answer questions. I could not have done the job without them. Mary Norris went further: she read the entire manuscript and interviewed Maida Springer shortly before Springer's death at age ninety-five. Eric Springer came to Chapel Hill to tell me about growing up as Pauli Murray's protégé, and Emily Herring Wilson and Ruth Emerson shared their memories of Pauli. Without Kate Torrey, Ron Maner, Catherine Fagan, David Perry, and other members of the UNC Press staff, you would not be reading this book today.

Judy Bellin and Will Scott did some of the boring work of proofreading to make sure the transcripts were accurate. Larry Smith, Ross Mc-Kinney, Judy Bellin, and Anne Geer, with remarkable tolerance for my ignorance, made my computer behave when it baffled me.

As has been the case for more than forty years, Marie Alston Lee provided the essential backup on the home front.

Andrew Scott made major contributions; sadly, he died before the final draft. The book would have been better organized and more insightful had he lived another year. I dedicate it to him in gratitude for fifty-eight years of collaboration in many things and to our grandchildren, who were so dear to him. To all the above I say a heartfelt thank you, with the usual mea culpa for all the sins of omission and commission.

Anne Firor Scott
Chapel Hill, North Carolina

National Association for the Advancement of Colored People (NAACP), 17, 19, 57, 86, 105, 167
National Defense Advisory Commission, 10, 23
National Organization for Women (NOW), 138, 144, 146, 155
National Urban League, 16–17
New Deal, 6, 8, 78, 185
New York City Department of Social Services, 78–80
New York Liberal Party, 47, 52
Nixon, Richard, 154–55
Norris, Mary, 148, 161, 163–64, 186–87
Norton, Eleanor Holmes, 168

Office of Price Administration (OPA), 11, 44
Opportunity, 17
Oxford University, 3, 35, 171–73

Paul, Weiss, Rifkind, Wharton, and Garrison (law firm), 108–11
Plessy v. Ferguson, 33, 60–61
PM, 25, 26, 28
President's Commission on the Status of Women (Kennedy administration), ix, 137
Proud Shoes (Murray), x, 21, 83–85, 99, 104, 106, 149, 165

"Question of Identity" (Murray), 123, 125, 128

Radcliffe College, 3
Ransom, Leon, 20, 164
Richmond Hill High School (New York City), 14

Rifkind, Simon H., 109, 164
Roosevelt, Eleanor, ix, 53, 104–5, 137, 141; and Murray, 15, 18, 19–20, 21, 27, 63, 66, 67, 73, 98, 110, 149–50, 152, 164; and Ware, 21, 27, 141, 158; in *Eleanor and Franklin*, 158
Roosevelt, Franklin D., 6, 17–18, 21, 23, 26, 35, 41, 158
Rosenwald Scholarship, 26

Salmon, Lucy Maynard, 2
Salzburg Seminar, 114, 132–33
San Francisco Conference, 36
Scott, Andrew, 182
Segregation, 13, 23, 45
Sexual identity, 14
Sit-ins, 20
Smith, Hilda Worthington, 2, 16, 165, 183
Smith, Lillian, 28n, 99, 101–2
Smith family (Murray's ancestors), 12, 16, 85
Snelling, Paula, 28n
Song in a Weary Throat (Murray), 153, 162, 167
South Today, 28
Springer, Eric, 82–83, 88
Springer, Maida, 47, 56, 58, 66–70, 79, 81, 104, 135, 167, 168; as Murray's close friend, 47n, 55, 91, 121; relationship with Ware, 55, 114, 120, 122, 126, 130, 168, 181; and Africa, 72, 77, 82, 113, 121, 126, 127; health of, 90, 122, 131
States' Laws on Race and Color (Murray), 51, 54, 62, 66, 72, 90, 96–97
Stevenson, Adlai, 15, 76, 104–6, 141
Supreme Court, 19, 33, 155–58

Truman, Harry, 41, 42, 60; Fair Deal of, 49

UNESCO. See *History of Mankind: Cultural and Social Development*, vol. VI, *The Twentieth Century*
United Nations Secretariat, 72–73
University of North Carolina at Chapel Hill, 17, 20, 27, 67, 152, 165–66, 173–79, 181

Vassar College, 1, 2, 5, 6, 24, 26–27, 184
Virginia Theological Seminary, 164

Wallace, Henry, 41, 42
Waller, Odell, 19–20, 181
Williams, Frances, 53
Women's Society for Christian Service, 44, 54, 56
Workers Defense League, 19, 25
Workers' education, 2, 3, 27
World War II, 23

Yale University, 134–36, 140–43
Yellow Head Island (Ware-Means residence), 119, 159, 164